Elsie Inglis

Elsie Inglis

Founder of battlefield hospitals run entirely by women

Leah Leneman

NMS Publishing

Published by
NMS Publishing Limited
Royal Museum, Chambers Street, Edinburgh EH1 1JF

© Leah Leneman and NMS Publishing Limited 1998
Index © Stephanie Pickering 1998

Series editor: Iseabail Macleod

Other titles available in this series
   The Gentle Lochiel
Forthcoming titles
   Miss Cranston
   Mungo Park

Other titles by the author include
   *Into the Foreground: Scottish
      Women in Photographs*

**British Library Cataloguing
in Publication Data**
A catalogue record of this book is available
from the British Library

ISBN 1 901663 09 4

Cover design by NMS Publishing
Typeset by Artisan Graphics, Edinburgh
Printed in the UK by J W Arrowsmith Ltd

ACKNOWLEDGEMENTS

The earlier biographies which I drew on are listed in the Bibliography. Unpublished source material at the Mitchell Library, Fawcett Library, Imperial War Museum and elsewhere is acknowledged and fully referenced in my book *In the Service of Life*. Once again, my thanks to all. Material on the Bruntsfield Hospital and The Hospice is available in Lothian Health Services Archive, Edinburgh, and I am grateful for the 'probationer's memories' supplied by that archive.

Graham Sutton's editorial hand has made the text which follows more readable, and discussing Elsie Inglis with him helped to enhance my own interpretation of her character and achievements. His help, as always, was invaluable.

Illustrations

Cover: Douglas, Davidson and Chisholm tartans. Swatches kindly lent by the Clan Tartan Centre of James Pringle Weavers, through the good offices of James McAslan.

8: Scottish National Portrait Gallery
22: courtesy of Amy Maddox
35, 36, 41, 63: National Museums of Scotland
46: from *Dr Elsie Inglis* by Lady Frances Balfour
52: from *Shadow of Swords* by Margot Lawrence
70: from *Shadow of Swords* by Margot Lawrence
76: by kind permission of Audrey Cahill

Introduction

'Born in the Elsie Inglis' — that is how her name is recalled. From 1925 until 1988 generations of Edinburgh babies were born in the Elsie Inglis Memorial Hospital, and there was a fading folk memory that she had been a pioneer lady doctor who set up a hospital in the city for women and children. With the building surviving as the Elsie Inglis Nursing Home, and the Elsie Inglis maternity ward in the Western General Hospital, the name at least will linger on. Elsie Inglis is a woman commemorated for the second most important thing she ever did.

It was not because of her contribution to Edinburgh's maternity services that news of her death in 1917 caused national shock and grief. Her body lay in state in St Giles' Cathedral; the Queen sent a message of condolence to her sister; her funeral in Edinburgh was followed by a memorial service in Westminster where members of parliament, government ministers, British diplomats, heads of Red Cross and Army Medical Services, representatives of French, Italian and Russian embassies and Serbian, Belgian, and Rumanian legations, lords, ladies, suffragists, army and navy officers, and many other distinguished people paid homage to her, when the Bishop of Oxford said they 'were met to commemorate a truly glorious woman', who 'exhibited in the highest degree a combination of personal self-sacrifice and tenderest sympathy, with a rare capacity for origination and government.' Clearly Elsie Inglis did something more than open a maternity hospital.

Dr Elsie Maud Inglis 1864–1917. Bronze bust by Ivan Mestrovic.

The date provides the clue. 'The story of the last three years of Dr Elsie Inglis's life is a remarkable record of a Scotswoman's war work', proclaimed the Glasgow *Bulletin*. And in *The Scotsman* of 28 November 1917: 'Widespread sorrow will be felt at the announcement of the death of Dr Elsie Inglis, the founder of the Scottish Women's Hospitals for Foreign Service. Since the early days of the war, her name has been made familiar in connection with beneficent work in many lands. It will take a high place amongst the records of heroic service in the great struggle... In Serbia and elsewhere, Scotland is associated with the work of Dr Elsie Inglis and her colleagues on the battlefield and behind the lines, where they tended the wounded and helped to succour the helpless. Dr Inglis was not only the intrepid and inspiring leader on the actual scene of the work; her enthusiasm, energy, and experience were to a large extent the motive power which has created a vast organisation, of which, as a voluntary effort and an expression of humanity, any country might be proud.'

During the First World War Elsie Inglis carved for herself a niche in the national consciousness. She created a unique organisation that captured the public imagination so fully it seems astonishing how completely it has been forgotten. Her obituarist in *The Lancet* wrote: 'Elsie Inglis gave her life for her country and its allies as truly as any soldier in the trenches has ever done and as cheerfully. She was a wonderful compound of enthusiasm, strength of purpose, and kindliness, a threefold blend exactly calculated to allow full play to her great organising abilities. Remarkably modest, she was always full of generous appreciation of others. In the history of this world-war, alike by what she did and by the heroism, driving-power, and simplicity with which she did it, Elsie Inglis has earned an everlasting place of honour.'

Two-thirds of this book are devoted to the last three years of Elsie Inglis' life; were it not for those last three years it would never have been written at all. Elsie Inglis' name might have graced a plaque in a hospital corridor, but her story would lack the drama and heroism granted it by the extraordinary circumstances of the Great War. Creating an all-woman organisation that sent over a thousand women to the Front as doctors, nurses, orderlies, drivers; herself organising medical services in Serbia, and continuing to care for patients under German occupation; evading enemy capture while taking part in no less than three retreats in Rumania and refusing to go until the last possible moment; holding her unit together amid the tumult of the Russian Revolution while in the grip of terminal illness. . . Those years were the culmination of her life, when what was best (and, occasionally, worst) in her character came to the fore. The honour accorded to her on her death was well deserved, and her story is worth the telling.

1

Elsie Maud Inglis was born in India during the heyday of the British Empire, on 16 August 1864. Her father, John Inglis, descended from the Inglis family of Kingsmills, near Inverness, was born in 1820, and went out as a young member of the East India Company as assistant magistrate at Agra. In 1845 Harriet Thompson, aged seventeen, whose father was a longstanding member of the Indian Civil Service, came to join her family. She met John Inglis at a dance in her father's house, and the two hit it off immediately. She was a fine rider and an intrepid character, accepting with equanimity all the dangers and discomforts of travelling around India. The following year (1846) she married John.

Both John and Harriet had a strong religious faith, which created a bond between them and was passed on to their children. It was not a narrow or parochial faith; they were members of the Anglican Church in India and later in Edinburgh joined the Free Church of Scotland, and were happy to worship wherever convenient. Neither was it mystical nor proselytising; it was simply a firm, practical belief in God and the power of goodness and right.

In 1847 John was transferred to the newly-acquired province of the Punjab, serving as magistrate to Sealkote until 1856. By this time the couple had a family of five — four boys and a girl — and Harriet was pregnant with a sixth. John was due a three-year furlough, and after a four-month overland trek in relays of hired bullock wagons, followed by a four-month sea voyage to England round the Cape, the family reached Southampton — only to learn that mutiny had broken out in India. John was recalled and stayed just long enough to see Harriet through the birth of their sixth child, before going back to play his part in the suppression of the Mutiny. For the next six years it was considered unsafe for British women to go to India, so Harriet had to stay in Southampton with her children, separated by thousands of miles from her husband.

When she sailed from England to India in 1863 Harriet had another separation to face, for it was considered right to leave the children behind, the older boys in public schools, and Amy, the only girl (with whom Harriet had a particular bond), and the youngest boy, Ernest, in the care of relatives. One of the children born after Harriet's return to India was convinced that her mother 'left her heart behind with the six elder children'. However, now there was reunion with her lonely husband, and the begetting of a second family, starting with Elsie Maud. There were two further children, Eva and Horace, but from the beginning Elsie, a symbol of a hopeful new era in his life, was special to John.

As an infant Elsie had to adapt to long expeditions with her parents, and her mother reported her as 'accommodating herself to circumstances, watching the trees, sleeping under them, and the jolliest little traveller I ever saw.' Four months after the birth Harriet wrote that Elsie was 'very well, but she is a very little thing with a very wee face. She has a famous pair of large blue eyes, and it is quite remarkable how she looks about her and seems to observe everything.' Harriet thought that 'she is one of the most intelligent babies I ever met with.'

The setting for Elsie's birth was Naini Tal, a beautiful hill station in the Himalayas. Above them stretched wooded slopes rich in flowers and wildlife, and above that again towered snow-capped majestic peaks. Eva always remembered the glorious after-breakfast walks with their father. 'We got equal shares of his right and his left hand', she wrote, 'but Elsie and he were comrades, inseparables from the day of her birth.' (But there was no jealousy, she insisted, because 'Father was always just'.) And there was also their 'quiet strong mother'. Every morning, before breakfast and the walk, the children would sit in front of her in a row and read the scripture verses, then kneel in a straight row and repeat the prayers after her. There was none of the segregation and relegation to the care of servants found in some Victorian homes: although there was a beloved ayah, Sona (who had travelled to England with the first family, stayed behind with Harriet, and then returned to nurse the second family), Harriet never banished her children to a nursery, and John, when he was at home, was an adoring father.

As the eldest of the 'second family' Elsie was their leader, organising their games and expected to set a good example. Eva had a particularly strong memory of one incident involving their dolls, all forty of them: 'Elsie decreed once that they should all have measles — so days were spent by us three painting little red dots all over the forty faces and the forty pairs of arms and legs. She was the doctor and prescribed gruesome drugs which we had to administer. Then it was decreed that they should slowly recover, so each day so many spots were washed off until the epidemic was wiped out!'

In 1858 the British Crown had replaced the East India Company as governors of India, and John Inglis's career in what was now the Indian Civil Service advanced steadily. In 1868 he was appointed a member of the Board of Revenue in the North-West Provinces. As a member of the Legislative Council of India, he moved, in 1873, to Calcutta. From 1875 to 1877 he was Chief Commissioner of Oude. The family moved in exalted circles, close friends of the Foreign Secretary of India, the Commander-in-Chief of the Army, and similar notables.

In common with other British families, they lived in the plains during the winter months and in the hills during the summer. From the time she was eleven, when separated from her father, Elsie would correspond with him by letter. When they were old enough to understand, the children were told that they had brothers and a sister in England as well, and in fact when Elsie was four her older sister Amy travelled to India to be married to Robert Simson of the Bengal Service, with the younger girls as bridesmaids.

Elsie had a gloriously happy and secure childhood. The family had a comfortable, even opulent existence (with no less than thirty servants in the household), but at the same time they truly believed in the idea of service; as privileged members of the British Empire they were convinced that they were bringing the highest possible civilisation to the country they ruled. This had always been the vision of the proconsul John Lawrence, of whom John Inglis was a devoted disciple, but things were changing in India. Russia was casting covetous looks via the Afghan border, and, with the appointment of Lord Lytton as Governor-General in November 1875, a much tougher imperialist line was being imposed, a viewpoint with which John Inglis was entirely out of sympathy. It had been expected that John would be promoted to Lieutenant-Governor of the North-West, but because of his views he was passed over for the post. It was the end of an era and, though only fifty-six, John decided there was no future for him in India. It was 1876 and time to retire.

He decided that Edinburgh was the place to go. Amy and her husband were planning to settle there, and the city had good day schools for girls, an attraction for John who had campaigned for female education in India and wanted it for his own daughters as well. Before travelling to Scotland, however, the family went to Tasmania. Two of the older Inglis boys, Hugh and Cecil, had proved 'unsatisfactory', and upper middle-class parents in this era shipped unsatisfactory progeny to the Australian colonies. Under-populated Tasmania, in particular, seemed to offer great opportunities for hard-working young men, and John took his younger family with him while the older boys 'settled in'. They were there for two years (and, in fact, the young men did not remain there long after their parents left them, drifting off to the Australian gold fields, and eventually disappearing entirely from the family's ken). There was plenty of fun for Elsie, Eva and Horace, and not only that but also schooling. A Miss Knott and her sister had gone to Hobart from the Cheltenham Ladies College where Dorothea Beale, one of the founders of education for women, was spreading the ideal of shaping educated women into a force to serve and uplift society.

Early in 1878 the Inglis family sailed for Great Britain. On board ship, while the two younger children played games, Elsie helped with the care of a baby, nursed sick children, and took charge of some 'turbulent' boys who lacked supervision and were making a nuisance of themselves to other passengers. At thirteen Elsie was already demonstrating key elements of her character. And to John Inglis, after his disappointments with his own career and with two of his sons, she was to become more important than ever.

In Edinburgh John Inglis found a suitable house at 70 Bruntsfield Place (the houses on that side of Bruntsfield Links, opposite the Bruntsfield Hotel, no longer exist, but others remain nearby to give a good impression of what it must have been like). Each day Elsie and Eva attended the Edinburgh Institution for the Education of Young Ladies at 23 Charlotte Square, a private school with a good reputation. The struggle for 'young ladies' to obtain higher education had largely been won by this time: London University opened its degrees to women that same year (1878), though other universities, including those in Scotland, took much longer.

However, even among those who supported their access to liberal arts, there was still resistance to medical training for women, despite the fact that many women so dreaded the attentions of a male doctor that they chose to suffer, and even die, in silence, rather than submit themselves to a physical examination by a man. It was the plight of those women, with whom Queen Victoria herself thoroughly sympathised, that in 1876 finally won for women the right to a medical degree. The redoubtable Sophia Jex-Blake, who had been at the forefront of the struggle, settled in Edinburgh the same year as the Inglis family, and as the first woman doctor in the city proved once and for all the great demand by women for a female practitioner. Already Elsie knew that that was what she was going to do: a schoolmate remembered many years later 'the funny little girl with quantities of straight hair, whose favourite lesson was Latin because she meant to be a doctor.'

One particular episode of her schooldays was remembered vividly by her classmates. Apart from the school all of the other houses in Charlotte Square were private dwellings, and their wealthy inhabitants had keys to the garden in the centre of the square. Pupils at the Institution, however, did not have permission to play there but were cooped indoors all day. They looked longingly at the green space forbidden to them, but only Elsie had the courage ('to us schoolgirls it seemed the extraordinary courage') to speak to the three directors of the school and ask if they might be allowed to play games there. Their answer was that the girls could do so if all the Charlotte Square proprietors agreed, so Elsie, with one companion, went to each house and asked the owner's consent, which again seemed amazingly brave to Victorian girls. Having got the consent of every householder, she returned triumphant, and the girls were able to enjoy much-appreciated breaks of fresh air and exercise.

In 1882, when Elsie was eighteen, it was decided that she would benefit from a year abroad, in Paris. John Inglis dreaded the 'weary time' while she was away, but he had sought 'the Lord's guidance' and believed that he and Harriet had 'been guided to do what was best for you'.

Elsie and six other girls were accompanied by a Miss Gordon Brown who chaperoned them and accompanied them home again in September 1883. Elsie visited all the sights of Paris, had lessons in drawing, music and singing, dancing, and, of course, French. None of the latter were of much avail, for Elsie had no ear for either music or languages. A niece later wrote that 'her musical capabilities became a family joke which no one enjoyed more than herself. She had two "pieces" which she could play by heart, of the regular arpeggio drawing-room style, and these always had to be performed at any family function as one of the standing entertainments.'

Elsie and her father carried on a vigorous correspondence while she was abroad, but he missed her greatly. At his wish she sent him a timetable of her days so he could follow her in thought. When she returned home she found that her mother, though only fifty-five, had become a frail old woman. Whatever medical ambitions Elsie might have had, she set them aside for the time being and contented herself with the life of most unmarried middle-class young women of the time: family gatherings, mission meetings, musical evenings and the like. In January 1885 this period ended when her mother died of scarlet fever. 'From that day', wrote her sister Eva, 'Elsie shouldered all father's burdens, and they two went on together until his death.'

The family moved (perhaps as an economy measure) to upper apartments in Melville Street, where Elsie kept house, an occupation not at all congenial to her. 'I must devote my mind more to the housekeeping' was one of a list of resolutions she made at that time. Others included: 'I must give up dreaming — making stories. I must give up getting cross. I must be more thorough in everything. I must be truthful.' And she concluded: 'The bottom of the whole evil is the habit of dreaming, which must be given up. So help me, God.' Whether her 'dreams' were of a medical career which she felt she could not consider while she was so needed by her father, or whether they were more romantic, and what made her think she was not 'truthful' enough, cannot be known, but the 'resolutions' reveal the kind of firm self-discipline she exercised throughout her life.

The compensation for her mundane existence at this time was an even greater closeness to her father. They took long walks and explored every topic under the sun. To have left him at this stage would have been inconceivable, but fortuitously, in 1886, it became feasible to begin medical training without having to do so. In that year (when the Medical Register contained the names of only fifty women) Dr Sophia Jex-Blake started her own small hospital in Edinburgh, and announced the opening of the Edinburgh School of Medicine for Women. Elsie told her father of her plan of 'going in for medicine', and he expressed himself entirely in favour of the idea. The fees were modest, she could live at home, and she would then be in a position to support herself for the rest of her life.

The idea of a woman receiving medical education in mixed classes was still abhorrent to society at large, and most received their training at the London School of Medicine for Women. That School had been founded on the initiative of Sophia Jex-Blake and Elizabeth Garrett Anderson, but Sophia's abrasive personality had antagonised too many people and she was edged out of that project. Now she was fulfilling her dream, and at first all went well, for J-B, as she was generally known, was a fine teacher, and her pupils were full of enthusiasm. But J-B's autocratic and over-controlling temperament soon began to irk them. Small incidents became magnified, such as strictly enforcing times of leaving Leith Hospital where they undertook some of their clinical training, no matter if an interesting case held them back.

Finally a row broke out over a Miss Sinclair who had failed an examination but, after prevailing on a lecturer to explain the circumstances to the examiner, obtained her certificate. J-B publicly accused her of dishonourable conduct; two sisters, Grace and Georgina Cadell, supported Miss Sinclair and were dismissed from the school for insubordination. They promptly brought an action for damages of £500 each. Elsie allied herself with the rebels, and became known as their leader, leading to 'awful rows' with those who supported J-B. Although many believed that J-B's struggles for medical women entitled her to more consideration than she then received, to Elsie the real issue was whether women students were to be recognised as mature individuals with the right to protest against injustices in the same way as men could.

The case was not heard in court until a year later, in summer 1889, when it was the talk of Edinburgh. The judge found in favour of the Cadell sisters but awarded them £50 each instead of the £500 they had claimed. However, by then Elsie had taken more radical action to break

J-B's monopoly on women's medical education outside London. The project was to establish an alternative medical school for women, and it quickly came to fruition. Elsie's father had influential friends, and Sophia had made many enemies. The new Medical College for Women was housed in rented premises at 30 Chambers Street. At first facilities were not as good as in J-B's school, and of course Leith Hospital was out of bounds, so that students had to travel to Glasgow Royal Infirmary for their hospital training. But fees were lower, and there were fewer restrictions. It opened for the winter term 1889/90, with eighteen distinguished lecturers, and with Elsie herself, the Cadell sisters, and more than enough other women enrolled to make it a viable concern. Within two years it had endowed two wards in the Edinburgh Royal Infirmary, previously a stronghold of anti-feminism, to be set aside for women students.

Before that happened Elsie went to Glasgow for her clinical training, her first time away from home since her mother's death. She stayed at a YWCA hostel and wrote to her father shortly after her arrival, on 4 February 1891, 'I am most comfortable here, and I am going to work like *anything*.' Her good fortune was in being there at the same time as William MacEwen (knighted in 1902), one of the greatest surgeons of the day. Not only was he an innovator in bone surgery, and one of the first to operate for brain disorders, he entirely lacked the prejudice against women so prevalent amongst his colleagues. He did not even feel the need to make concessions to them. 'This morning I spent the whole time in Dr MacEwen's wards', Elsie wrote to her father on 9 February; 'He put me through my facings. I could not think what he meant, he asked me so many questions. It seems it is his way of greeting a new student. Some of them cannot bear him, but I think he is really nice, though he can be abominably sarcastic, and he is a first-rate surgeon and capital teacher.'

Subsequently Elsie wrote that when she told William MacEwen about her wish to endow a women's college in Edinburgh, 'He said he thought that would be great waste; there should not be separate colleges. "If women are going to be doctors, equal with men, they should go to the same schools." I said I quite agreed with him, but when they won't admit you, what you are to do? "Leave them alone," he said; "they will admit you in time," and he thought outside colleges would only delay that.'

Ironically, a few months later Elsie and her fellow women students had a fight on their hands in Glasgow. Having paid their fees for the full course of medical tuition, they were told in November 'that we are not to go to mixed classes, and we have been tearing all over the wards seeing all sorts of people about it'. When they spoke to one doctor about it 'he hummed and hawed, looked everywhere except at us, and then said the Infirmary Managers said we were not to go to mixed classes. So I promptly said, "Then I shall come for my fees tomorrow," and walked out of the room. I was angry.' One doctor even threatened to prevent their attendance by 'physical force', thereby arming the students with yet another legal grievance. But Elsie realised that 'we cannot be beat here… Were the managers, managers a hundred times over, they cannot turn Mr MacEwen off'. MacEwen was decisively on their side, and the fight was won.

Her period in Glasgow exposed her for the first time to the lives of working-class women from slum dwellings, and what outraged her most was not the dirt and disorder but the exploitation. One woman who was in with a broken leg was 'a shirt finisher. She sews on the buttons and puts in the gores at the rate of $4\frac{1}{2}$d. a dozen shirts. We know the shop, and they sell the shirts at 4s. 6d. each. . . I hope that shopkeeper, if ever he comes back to this earth, will be a woman and have to finish shirts at $4\frac{1}{2}$d. a dozen, and then he'll see the other side of the question.' But Elsie was still naive: 'I told the woman it was her own fault for taking such small wages, at which she seemed amused.'

Elsie's later letters from Glasgow concerned her fears about the coming examinations. As expected by William MacEwen and everyone else who knew her, she passed with flying colours, and on 4 August 1892, as a Licentiate of the Royal College of Physicians and Surgeons, Edinburgh, and Licentiate of the Faculty of Physicians and Surgeons, Glasgow, her name was entered in the British Medical Register as a qualified doctor.

At this stage her medical career took precedence, and she was delighted to take up a post as resident medical officer at the New Hospital for Women in London. Elizabeth Garrett Anderson, while remaining a consultant, had just been succeeded as head by Mrs (later Dame) Mary Scharlieb, a brilliant doctor who had worked in India and was largely responsible for Queen Victoria's conversion to the idea of medical women. Apart from the fascination of the work, Elsie had a wonderful time exploring London. She was taken under the wing of Mrs Garrett Anderson, and there were various family members and family friends in the city to accompany her out and about. At the same time her link with her father, John, remained as strong as ever; from the moment she arrived she wrote to him every day.

'My own dearest Papa, — Here we begin another long series of letters. The people in the carriage were very quiet, so I slept all right. Of course they shut up all the windows, so I opened all the ventilators, and I also opened the window two or three times. I had breakfast at once, and then a bath, and then came in for a big operation by Mrs Boyd... I think I shall like being here very much. I only hope I shall get on with all my mistresses! And, I hope I shall always remember what to do.'

The injustices of women's position at every level continued to strike her: 'The last big operation case died. It was very sad, and very provoking, for she really was doing well, but she had not vitality enough to stand the shock. That was the case whose doctor told her and her husband that she was suffering from hysteria. And that man, you know, can be a fellow of the colleges, and member of any society he likes to apply to, while Mrs G. Anderson and Mrs Sharlieb cannot! Is it not ridiculous?'. Mrs Garrett Anderson was suggesting that Elsie took up a maternity post there. 'I shall come home first, however, my own dearest Papa. Mrs G.A. said she thought I should have a good deal more of that kind of work if I was going to set up in a lonely place like Edinburgh [sic], as I ought never to have to call in a man to help me out of a hole!'

Elsie's enthusiasm bubbles through her letters: 'Lovely weather here. I have been prescribing sunshine, sunshine, sunshine for all the patients. There are only two balconies on each floor, and nurse Rose is reported to have said that she supposed I wanted the patients hung out over the railings, for otherwise there would not be room.' No matter how junior she was, Elsie was still a critical observer. 'They are all most frightfully nervous about anaesthetics here, in all the hospitals', which, she believed was because 'they watch the wrong organ, viz. the heart. In Scotland they hardly think of the heart, and simply watch the breathing. The Hyderabad Commission settled conclusively that it was the breathing gave out first; but having made up their minds that it does not, all the Commissions in the world won't convince them to the contrary. In the meantime they do their operations in fear and trembling, continually asking if the patient is all right.' But she was also appreciative: 'You never saw such a splendid out-patient department as they have here... The patients have to pay a small sum, yet they had over 20,000 visits this year… Who says women doctors are not wanted!'

After a valuable year in London, and before returning to Edinburgh, Elsie decided that the place to gain more experience in midwifery was at the Rotunda in Dublin. Not only was it a centre of excellence, the teaching was in 'mixed' classes. She worked long hours, and was called out nights, but assured her father, 'I am not such an idiot as to miss my meals, Papa dearest. My temper won't stand it!' She always had a glass of milk and a biscuit when she went out at night and was 'as sensible as I can be. I know you cannot do work with blunt instruments, and this instrument blunts very easily without food and exercise.'

In February 1894 she wrote, 'After three months you have learnt all the Rotunda can teach. If you were a man, it would be worth while to stay, because senior students, if they are men, get a lot of the C.C.'s work to do. But they never think of letting you do it if you are a woman.' Still, she had 'learnt a tremendous lot here, and feel very happy about my work in this special line.' She had ideas about where else she might study — Paris again, perhaps? — but then out of the blue came a letter from a fellow student at the Jex-Blake school, Jessie MacGregor, who had remained loyal to Sophia and had been appointed as junior medical officer at J-B's small hospital. Jessie MacGregor suggested that they start a practice together in Edinburgh. Admittedly they had disagreed at the time of the J-B controversy, but 'that was not a personal question', and 'Miss MacGregor is a splendid pathologist.'

The more she thought about it, the more Elsie liked the idea, and she returned home at the beginning of March. During the preceding months she had occasionally expressed anxiety over her father's failing health, but he had concealed from her just how ill he really was, and there was only a short period of time for her to nurse him through his final days, for he died on 13 March. Two days later she wrote to her brother Ernest in India about their father's end: 'He always said that he did not believe that death was the stopping place, but that one would go on growing and learning through all eternity. God bless him in his onward journey. I simply cannot imagine life without him.'

Elsie Inglis in mourning.

2

There are not many 30-year-old women for whom the death of a father would be the greatest blow that life could bring, but John Inglis had been the lodestar of Elsie's existence, and it took her years to get over his death. Although a campaigner on women's issues, Elsie was never a man-hating feminist, and her relationships with men she respected were good. If there is not the slightest hint of any emotional involvement with anyone she met either professionally or socially, only part of this would have been due to her professional aspirations and ambitions. Every potential husband she met would have been compared with her father, and none would have lived up. Elsie could share with him all her thoughts and feelings, whether in person or by letter; she had his unstinting love and respect and, save only for sex and a family, it is difficult to see what any other man could have offered her. She did love children — that is testified by everyone who remembered her — but, apart from the many with whom she came in contact as a doctor (whose names and ages she astonished parents by remembering when they met her long afterwards), she had two married sisters with families in Edinburgh, and much of her life was centred on those families.

Some years afterwards (probably about 1906) Elsie began to write a novel, *The Story of a Modern Woman*, which was never seen by anyone in her lifetime. Though of no literary merit, it contains much that is autobiographical. In it she wrote of the way her heroine felt at the lowest ebb in her life: 'her bark seemed to be stranded among shallows. She felt that she was an old woman, and "second bests" her lot in the coming years. There could never be any life equal to the old life, in the backwater into which she had drifted.' But, as her heroine bounced back, so, too, did Elsie. Her life comprised three key spheres: work, family, and suffrage.

The women's suffrage movement in Britain had begun at the time of the Second Reform Act in 1867, when many more men but no women were granted the vote. The zeal of the early years gradually waned when it became clear that overcoming male resistance was going to be a long slog, but by the 1890s, with so many of the other campaigns (like women's rights to a higher education) already won, there was a stirring of enthusiasm and activity across the country. Societies in London, Edinburgh and elsewhere were united under a new umbrella, the National Union of Women's Suffrage Societies (NUWSS).

Already in 1891 Elsie wrote from Glasgow to her father about going round to see some of her patients and finding that a woman who should have been in bed had been up all night because her husband had come home drunk and was lying asleep on the bed. 'I think he ought to have been horse-whipped', she commented, 'and when I have the vote I shall vote that all men who turn their wives and families out of doors at eleven o'clock at night, especially when the wife is ill, shall be horse-whipped.' She was pleased with her father's stance on 'women's rights': 'You are ahead of all the world in everything, and they gradually come up into line with you'. As far as she was concerned, 'There is no question among women who have to work for themselves about wanting the suffrage. It is the women who are safe and sound in their own drawing-rooms who don't see what on earth they want it for.'

But it was her period in London, at the New Hospital for Women, that marked a turning point in her involvement. Elizabeth Garrett Anderson, founder of the hospital, had been involved in the early days of the suffrage campaign, and her sister, Millicent Garrett Fawcett, was president of the NUWSS, so a feminist consciousness pervaded the place. And her experience of working-class marriages was an eye-opener.

'I have just been so angry!', she began a letter to her father. A woman had come in and needed an operation, but her husband arrived at the hospital and said she was needed at home to look after the children, who had been crying. 'I said I saw very well what it was, that he had just had a bad night, and had just determined that his wife should have the bad night to-night, even though she was ill, instead of him. He did look ashamed of himself, selfish cad! Helpless creature, he could not even arrange for some one to come in and take charge of those children unless his wife went home to do it.' In spite of everything Elsie said, the woman went home, and Elsie wondered 'when married women will learn they have any other duty in the world than to obey their husbands... You don't know what trouble we have here with the husbands. They will come in the day before the operation, after the woman has been screwed up to it, and worry them with all sorts of outside things, and want them home when they are half dying. Any idea that anybody is to be thought of but themselves never enters their lordly minds, and the worst of it is these stupid idiots of women don't seem to think so either... They don't seem to think they have any right to any individual existence.'

'We have had another row with a tyrannical husband', she began a letter, 'I did not know whether to be most angry with him or his fool of a wife.' The woman had a very painful abscess on the breast, and Dr Helen Webb, the out-patient physician, wanted to admit her immediately, but her husband refused because he said the baby was not old enough to be left with anyone else. All appeals to him failed, and Elsie remarked, 'What a fool the woman must have been to have educated him up to that.' But she and Dr Webb struck up a great friendship as a result of the incident: 'After we had both fumed about for some time, I said "Well, the only way to educate that kind of man, or that kind of woman, is to get the franchise." Miss Webb said, "Bravo, bravo," then I found she was a great franchise woman'.

It was about this time that Elsie first spoke publicly on the subject. She had been asked by Mrs Wolstenholme Elmy, one of the earliest feminist campaigners, to speak to a drawing room meeting 'on the present state of medical education in the country' but 'thought that would be too great cheek in a house surgeon'. Having instead prepared a speech on suffrage, she arrived late to find a 'fearfully and awfully fashionable audience being harangued by a very smart-looking man, who spoke uncommonly well'. It was only as he was finishing that Elsie realised from the way Mrs Elmy smiled and nodded at her that she was expected simply to 'second the motion this man was speaking to.' And he had already said most of what she had meant to say! 'I was in such an awful funk that I got cool, and got up and told them that I did not think Mr Wilkins had left any single thing for me to say; however, as things struck people in different ways I should simply tell them how it struck me, and then went ahead with what I meant to say when I got in.' She received a good response ('Mrs Elmy said I had not repeated Mr W., only emphasised him'), which encouraged further participation.

One of the first three suffrage societies formed in 1867 was the Edinburgh National Society for Women's Suffrage, and it was still going strong in the 1890s when Elsie returned to the city. She became honorary secretary of the executive committee and formed new friendships. In her unpublished novel she wrote of her heroine: 'As she threw herself into this new interest she found a gale of fresh air blowing through her life. It was almost as if she had awakened on a new morning. The sunshine flooded every nook and corner of her dwelling, and some old things looked different in the new light. Not the least of these impressions was due to the new friendships; women whose life-work was farthest from her own, whose point of view was diametrically opposite to hers, suddenly drew up beside her in the march as comrades. She felt as if she had got a wider outlook over the world, as if in her upward climb she had reached a spur on the hillside, and a new view of the landscape spread itself at her feet.'

Meanwhile, her medical career absorbed most of her energy. The partnership with Dr Jessie MacGregor was a happy one, and they soon had a substantial practice, beginning in Atholl Place, but soon after moving to the fashionable Walker Street. While content to treat the rich, Elsie spent much of her time visiting poorer families. They adored her, naming their children after her and clubbing together to buy a torch for her to light the way up dark tenement stairs. Her care went far beyond prescribing medicine; she involved herself in the lives of families in need, personally sterilising milk in one home where three infants had died (the fourth, who got the sterilised milk, thrived), coming at night to bathe a baby when the mother was ill, even helping to raise money to send a poor woman to a sanatorium for six months. One man said: 'That woman has done more for the folk living between Morrison Street and the High Street than all the ministers in Edinburgh and Scotland itself ever did for anyone.'

Apart from her own practice, Elsie worked most mornings at one of the city's dispensaries (St Cuthbert's, St Anne's, Morrison Street, Little

Sisters of the Poor), or at the YWCA's section for unmarried mothers (euphemistically called the 'servant department'). A woman there at the time later wrote about the way Elsie's appearance would bring confidence to her 'when getting heartless over some of these poor creatures who would not rouse themselves, judging the world was against them. Many a time the patient fighting with circumstances needed a sisterly word of cheer which Dr Inglis supplied, and sent the individual heartened and refreshed. The expression on her face, *I mean business*, had a wonderful uplift'.

While still in London Elsie already had the idea of starting her own hospital, and back in Edinburgh she took the first step by forming a Medical Women's Club, of which she was the secretary and which usually met at Walker Street. In January 1899 Elsie heard that Sophia Jex-Blake was planning to modernise and extend her Edinburgh Hospital for Women and Children (later known as the Bruntsfield Hospital), and then retire and hand it over to trustees. Elsie wrote with an offer of money but only on condition that the Medical Club had fifty percent representation on the committee. The offer was refused, so Elsie returned to the idea of starting her own hospital. She launched an appeal, and persuaded the owner of a property at 11 George Square to let it to them at a nominal rent. The modest hospital of seven beds was opened in November.

Toward the end of 1903 the lease on the George Square hospital was running out, and new premises had to be found. As far as Elsie was concerned, the most valuable work they were doing was among the poor, so she chose a property on the High Street and named it The Hospice. Opening in January 1904, it was a surgical and gynaecological centre with its own operating theatre, and was also a centre for district midwifery. In addition there was a general dispensary and accident department, and it was so successful that in December a resident medical officer, Dr Alice Hutchison, was appointed.

As soon as the admission book showed a steady intake of patients Elsie applied for, and got, recognition as a lecturer for the Central Midwifery Board, which meant that she could admit resident pupils (nurses and students) to The Hospice for practical instruction in midwifery. Dr Alice Hutchison was 'second in command', and other staff members included Dr Grace Cadell (prime mover in the rebellion against Sophia Jex-Blake) and Dr Beatrice Russell who ran the Infant Welfare Department.

A probationer at The Hospice from 1906 to 1908 (Marie Agnes Davies) remembered that 'the hospital was very poor and equipment very expensive so great economy had to be exercised in every department but Dr Inglis made sure that the patients had the best that the money would run to.' The hours were long and the work was hard but 'very rewarding'. Dr Inglis, who gave them lectures and instruction, 'was exacting as to details and was severe about careless mistakes but so ready with praise and encouragement for good work done.' Her 'vitality was felt by everyone. We were all afraid of her but also loved her for her kindness and humanity.'

'She worked at The Hospice with devotion', wrote Elsie's sister, Eva; 'Though cherishing always her aim of an institution which, while serving the poor, should provide a training for women doctors, she threw herself heart and soul into the work because she loved it for its own sake, and she loved her poor patients.'

Her practical knowledge of the poor led Elsie to undertake research into their nutrition, a new field, and she persuaded the town council to fund this, again an innovation at the time. In the resulting publication (*Study of the Diet of the Labouring Classes in Edinburgh*), produced in collaboration with two medical men, she concluded that 'the steady, thrifty poor who feel the difficulty of making both ends meet would appreciate and would benefit by simple instruction on the rules of diet.'

In 1905 Dr Jessie MacGregor decided to go to America for family reasons. Elsie was sufficiently established to keep 8 Walker Street on alone, and in July the Bruntsfield Hospital offered her the post vacated by Dr MacGregor. Sophia Jex-Blake had blocked an appointment of Elsie Inglis to a vacancy in 1901, and when she got heard of this offer she threatened to resign (she was still a consultant) if the appointment went through. But on this occasion the committee simply expressed regret at the severance of Sophia's connection with the hospital she had founded, and the appointment of Elsie Inglis, because of 'her ability and outstanding position amongst the women doctors of Edinburgh', went ahead.

That year also heralded a crucial change in the women's suffrage movement in Britain. Until then the only tactics used had been 'constitutional' ones, like petitions and patient lobbying. In 1905 Emmeline Pankhurst, a widow, and her daughters, frustrated at the lack of progress, instigated 'militancy', which at the beginning simply meant shouting 'Votes for Women', and heckling at political meetings in the way that men had always done, plus marching to the House of Commons. The Pankhursts were adept at gaining publicity, and suddenly women's suffrage was newsworthy. Not everyone in favour of votes for women favoured militancy, but thousands of women who had never even thought of the issue became aware of it and were eager to become involved. This, in turn, gave enormous impetus to the existing, 'constitutional' societies, which gained many new members, as well as new ideas. They may have decried the tactics of the militants ('suffragettes'), but the 'suffragists' also became a presence at political rallies.

Now there were meetings to be addressed all over the country, paid organisers to be employed and supervised, marches and processions to coordinate. There was far more time and energy needed, but also excitement and hope. Elsie made the heroine of her novel a suffragist and wrote: 'Not the least part of the interest of the new life was the feeling of being at the centre of things. People whose names had been household words since babyhood became living entities. She not only saw the men and women who were moulding our generation; she met them at tea, she talked intimately with them at dinners, and she actually argued with them at Council meetings.' And the way in which 'the Cause' transcended its nominal object is also illustrated in her heroine's thoughts: 'The salvation of the world was wrapped up in the gospel she preached. Many of the audience were caught up in the swirl as she spoke. Love and amity, the common cause of healthier homes and happier people and a stronger Empire, the righting of all wrongs, and the strengthening of all rights — all this was wrapped up in the vote.'

If Elsie herself spoke in that way it is not surprising that she inspired audiences, and at the same time she had so many real, everyday examples of injustices to draw on. At one meeting, to which she came, as she often did, straight from her practice, she illustrated her argument by something that had occurred the same day. The law did not permit an operation on a married woman without her husband's consent. A husband had that very day refused his consent, 'and the woman was to be left to lingering suffering from which only death could release her.' Lady Frances Balfour, a co-worker in the cause who was there that night, always remembered 'the voice and the thrill which pervaded speaker and audience as Dr Inglis told the tale and pointed the moral'. And Elsie could also inspire other workers. One evening Miss Bury, recruited by Elsie to organise suffrage societies in the Highlands, regretted that the hall was not full. Elsie's reply was, 'My dear, I was not counting the people, I was thinking of the efforts which had brought those who were there.'

By 1909 there was so much activity in Scotland that an umbrella organisation under the NUWSS, the Scottish Federation of Women's Suffrage Societies, was created to encompass all the non-militant societies, and Elsie became honorary secretary of that as well. Lady Frances Balfour wrote that in the early years of her professional life Elsie used 'to forecast for herself a large and paying practice.' After the explosion of suffrage activity 'her patients never suffered, but she sacrificed her professional prospects in a large measure for her work for the franchise. She gave her time freely, and she raised money at critical times by parting with what was of value and in her power to give.' And while Elsie remained entirely loyal to the non-militants, there is no suggestion of any rift with Dr Grace Cadell, who followed a different path.

Indeed, in 1907 when the senior consultant at the Bruntsfield Hospital retired, and Elsie succeeded to the post, at her suggestion Dr Cadell was brought in, not under her as would be usual but as co-equal. The arrangement may have been because of all the time and effort Elsie was committing to the suffrage campaign. However, the following year she began lecturing on gynaecology under the auspices of the University of Edinburgh's extramural department, and, together with Dr Beatrice Russell, she also began lecturing to the new Voluntary Visitors Association.

In October 1909, when Elsie was forty-five and without question Edinburgh's foremost woman doctor, an incident occurred — foreshadowing something similar that would happen a few years later — in which she nearly threw away the fruits of her success. The Bruntsfield Hospital was found guilty in a lawsuit over alleged negligence by a nurse, and the judge declared that the hospital committee had approved a letter which was 'not fair and honest', seemingly determined to clear itself at all costs. Elsie was not personally involved but was so incensed when the hospital did not appeal against the judgment that she tendered her resignation. Members of the hospital committee had not backed up their staff, 'and from that view alone' she could not longer work with them: 'But apart from that I do not think that anyone, or any body of people like the committee, are doing right when they allow such statements to be made about them without protest. There are some things which if they are not denied, are admitted, and these statements about the methods of the committee were made not by an irresponsible newspaper, but by a judge from the Bench. The only way of contradicting him is by appealing against his judgment. The committee obviously do not agree with me and feeling as strongly as I do on the point, the only course left to me is to resign.'

Her letter nowhere acknowledged the serious repercussions such a resignation would have had. The decision was hers, it was a point of principle, and that was that. Naturally the committee were appalled; the consequences to their work would have been disastrous. A compromise was suggested to her by Margaret Houldsworth, a committee member and fellow suffragist: if details of her protest were placed on the record, would she withdraw her resignation? Before Elsie had time to respond Miss Houldsworth suddenly died, leaving £3,000 'for the advantage of medical women and in pursuit of gynaecology and midwifery'. This opened up a new future for women's medical services; Elsie was reconciled with the committee and agreed to carry on.

The committee had decided to use the Houldsworth bequest to unite the two women's hospitals. The Bruntsfield Hospital would be enlarged so that all medical and surgical cases could be treated there, leaving The Hospice responsible for maternity and child welfare work only. In February 1911 the work was complete and the amalgamation took place. In July Queen Mary, on her coronation visit to Edinburgh, was proudly shown round the hospital, with its new surgical unit, by Dr Inglis.

The later years of the suffrage campaign, between 1912 and the outbreak of war in 1914, were difficult ones. Militancy in its milder phases had failed to break the deadlock, and angry, frustrated suffragettes turned to stone throwing and then to arson and home-made bombs, resulting in imprisonment, hunger strikes, and forcible feeding. They were still very newsworthy but had lost touch with public opinion, and the law-abiding suffragists were being tarnished by actions they themselves deplored.

Elsie had a break in 1913 when she went to America to see how medical women fared there and wrote enthusiastic letters full of ideas for further developments to The Hospice. On her return in September she was clearly unwell, and friends and colleagues urged her to take things more easily.

However, her life was never all work and campaigning, with no leisure. She always had September as a holiday, and for the first fortnight of the month she would take her bicycle, alone and without a forwarding address, to somewhere off the beaten track. She would pick a destination and when she got there would cycle around until she found somewhere she fancied staying. (Hot water for baths was the top priority.) She took her paintbox with her and brought back to her family sketches of scenes that appealed to her. The rest of the month would be spent with friends and family. (Apart from her two sisters and their children, when her brother Ernest died in India in 1910 his widow and her three daughters also came to Edinburgh). The younger generation of Simsons were now grown up, some of them married, and great-nephews and great-nieces were growing up alongside the young McLarens and Inglises. There were family members of an age to go on rambles and play golf with her, and others young enough to be read bedtime stories.

Sunday, whenever possible, was a day of rest. After evening service she always dined at the Simson house, and a niece later wrote about how much they all looked forward 'to hearing all her doings in the past week, and of all that lay before her in the next. Sunday evening felt quite wrong and flat when she was called out to a case and could not come to us.'

At this time, with a close family network, professional recognition and satisfaction, and a part to play in a movement which had brought her the comradeship of women whom she greatly admired and respected, it seemed she had it all. But she was tired. All that campaigning, now so disheartening with militants and government dug into irreconcilable positions and the vote seemingly further away than ever, and all the hard work and irregular hours of a career in obstetrics, were getting to be too much for a woman of fifty who was more seriously ill than she confessed to anyone at that time.

The Great War changed everything. In August 1914 she had little more than three years to live, but they were amazing years, for she founded a unique organisation and served on the field of battle.

3

After two Balkan wars in the previous two years, and belligerent posturings by the Germans and the Austro-Hungarian empire, the outbreak of war in August 1914 was not entirely unexpected. Even among the civilian population some preparations had been made: the Voluntary Aid Detachment movement started in 1909, and large numbers of women — themselves called VADs — learnt first aid, stretcher drill, and how to set up temporary hospitals. Elsie Inglis, as Commandant of an Edinburgh Voluntary Aid Detachment, was one of many women anticipating the possibility of war, and to play a part in it. What did take people aback was the timing and speed with which one outrage in the Balkans plunged all the European great powers into war.

The suffrage organisations reacted diversely to the outbreak of war. The Pankhursts disbanded their organisation, with Emmeline and Christabel throwing themselves wholeheartedly into the war effort. The NUWSS switched to relief work but retained its organisational structure, ready to step forward (as it did in 1917) whenever the suffrage campaign could resume. The continuing existence of that organisation provided the foundation for Elsie's wartime achievements.

Although she was nearly fifty, and her surgical experience had been virtually all in the field of gynaecology, she did not at first anticipate any difficulty in finding a post, so great must be the need. She heard that Elizabeth Garrett Anderson's daughter, Louisa, was forming a field hospital unit and wrote to her, but the unit was already complete. Elsie therefore went to Edinburgh Castle and offered her services to the RAMC, only to be rebuffed with the words, 'My good lady, go home and sit still'. There was nothing personal in this; men considered war to be their business, not that of the 'weaker' sex. Even two years later, when the shortage of male doctors was so acute that medical women had to be recruited, they were kept well away from the front line and were never granted officer status, despite all pleas for this. However, in this shambolically managed war there were opportunities for *ad hoc* efforts, and the Scottish Women's Hospitals for Foreign Service was the most substantial of those.

The idea in Elsie's mind had three motives: the first was patriotism, the second to demonstrate that medical women need not be restricted to gynaecology and paediatrics, and third, to prove women's fitness for the vote. No doubt it was this third argument that she stressed to the executive committee of the Scottish Federation of Women's Suffrage Societies, when she suggested that the Federation should offer the Red Cross a fully equipped hospital unit staffed by women. The committee agreed, but the Red Cross was in the hands of the War Office, which would not consider it. So the units were offered to Allied governments who might not be so resistant to the idea of medical women.

Such an enterprise required money, and on 12 September the NUWSS journal, the *Common Cause*, announced an appeal for £100 to provide a mobile hospital for work at the front: 'Already donations of over £12 have been received. Several women doctors, nurses and dressers have volunteered their services, and one lady has offered to go as interpreter.' Elsie pointed out in the next issue that what was needed was 'more like £1,000 than the £100 you so kindly beg for us.' This was based on an estimate of a unit of a hundred beds, with two senior and two junior doctors, ten nurses, and ten auxiliary staff, for six months. 'We might as well ask for a million at once', groaned one committee member, but Elsie went on to suggest a national appeal with a target of £50,000. By the beginning of October there were tentative plans of two hospitals, one for France and one for Serbia, but only £213 had been raised. However, a thousand copies of an appeal were sent throughout Scotland, and at a mass meeting on 'What Women Can Do to Help the War' at the Kingsway Hall, London, on 20 October, Elsie proclaimed her vision of sending out doctors, nurses, ambulance drivers wherever they were needed: 'The need

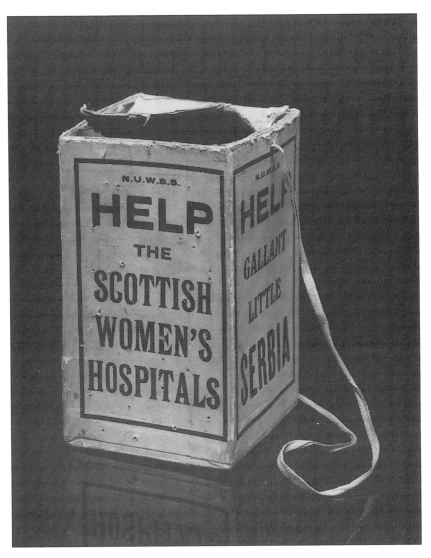

Collecting box for Scottish Women's Hospitals.

Red Cross Work in Calais, Malta and Serbia.

A

LANTERN LECTURE

WILL BE GIVEN ON

FRIDAY, JANUARY 28TH, 1916,

At 8 p.m.,

In the TRUSTEES HALL,

BOSTON SPA.

CHAIRMAN : THE REV. R. G. GLENNIE, M.A.

LECTURER :

DR. MARY PHILLIPS

Who will give an account of her **Personal Experience**
of Hospital work in CALAIS, MALTA and SERBIA,
and of a visit to SALONICA. (Numerous Slides).

TICKETS - 1s. and 6d.

To be obtained of Mrs. PERCY BOWNAS, or at the DOOR OF THE HALL.
DOORS OPEN AT 7-30 P.M.

PROCEEDS to go to the **RELIEF OF SERBIAN REFUGEES** in Corsica,
South of France, and Southern Italy.

Poster for a fundraising lecture by a Scottish Women's Hospitals' doctor, 1916.

is there, and too terrible to allow any haggling about who does the work.'
The money began to pour in.

Elsie was not herself in favour of the name 'Scottish Women's
Hospitals'. She wanted the organisation to have the widest possible appeal
and vetoed any suggestion that the word 'suffrage' appear in the title.
That point was won, but her suggestion of 'British Women's Hospitals'
was overruled by the Scottish Federation committee. The SWH committee
evolved from a sub-committee of the Scottish Federation in Edinburgh
into an entity of its own, organising personnel, press and publicity,
equipment, and transport. Its chairman was Mrs Nellie Hunter, a member
of the Glasgow and West of Scotland Association for Women's Suffrage
executive committee. Its treasurer was Mrs Jessie Laurie, who lived in
Greenock and was also the Scottish Federation treasurer; she was very
efficient, and at the same time a warm, motherly figure who was able to
see all sides of a question. A committee was also set up in London.

The idea and inspiration for the Scottish Women's Hospitals was
Elsie's, but much of the work, both in fund-raising and in organising the
units, had to be carried out by others. Tensions were soon manifest. On
30 December Alice Crompton, the organising secretary, wrote to Mrs
Laurie, 'Please let me have back as soon as convenient the draft Appeal.
Dr Inglis seems to be getting rather distressed because it is not already in
print and circulated.' On 24 February she wrote: 'Dr Inglis is very much
upset indeed because the Appeals are not ready yet. I do not think she
ever quite realised that it was a big business getting out all the Subscription
Lists.' Whatever the rights and wrongs of the particular point at issue, a
committee-run enterprise was never going to forge ahead at the speed
Elsie desired.

However, by 30 October 1914 the first £1,000 had already been raised.
At that stage only the Belgian government had accepted with enthusiasm
the offer of a hospital unit, and that country was already under enemy
occupation, but on 7 November the French accepted the offer, and on
the 8th the Serbs also did so. France's need was very apparent, with 300,000
of its soldiers killed in the first month of the war, while Serbia, which had
done its best to avoid the war, was seen as a David facing the Goliath of
Austria-Hungary. Money continued to roll in, and units were planned for
both countries. Dr Alice Hutchison was to negotiate the establishment of
a hospital in France, but when she arrived in Calais typhoid fever had

broken out amongst the Belgian refugees there, and help was asked of the SWH. With a junior doctor, a nursing sister, and ten more nurses, Dr Hutchison formed the first — very successful, albeit very short-lived — SWH hospital.

With Dr Hutchison hard at work in Calais, Elsie took her place in finding suitable premises for the French hospital. 'Suitable' might not have been the obvious word for the medieval abbey of Royaumont, twenty-five miles from Paris. Although the building was intact, most of it was disused, and the effort needed to convert it into a functioning hospital was immense. The first unit members crossed the Channel on 4 December, and, because neither the equipment nor beds had yet arrived, most of them had to carry straw mattresses with them from Paris to the abbey. But on her return from visiting it in December Elsie wrote to the organising secretary en route back to Folkestone: 'I do wish you could all see Royaumont for yourselves — it is *perfect*... it will be one of the finest Hospitals in France.'

That letter written from the ferry actually started with a complaint about the uniforms. It had been decided that they should be Scots grey with tartan facings, with the committee left to order the material and get them made up: 'We have been *thoroughly* done over them, — and I want the Committee as soon as possible to meet about it... The stuff is shoddy, and sewing coming undone... We were told we were paying 5/- a yard for that stuff — which I have no doubt we were, but that it was worth 5/- a yard is simply not the case. Imagine coats and skirts that are not fit to be seen after a month's wear.' And, turning from the subject of uniforms, she added: 'Dear Miss Crompton, we *must* plan something between us by which a *move* is kept on things.' More than two years later, in April 1917, when Elsie was out in Rumania, Mrs Laurie wrote to another committee member who was visiting a unit in Corsica, 'Things are just in their usual status quo. We miss Dr Inglis for a little vim and push.'

There were plenty of teething problems at Royaumont, including some disastrous initial staff appointments. The matron, for example, had come out of retirement to take up the post and could not cope. When Elsie visited the hospital in April she 'cried twice while talking to me, once on the stairs, and then again when I went to see her in her own room.' Elsie advised Mrs Laurie that 'she would gladly come home, if she could do so with honour. I think that is the only thing that is in the way.

She told me her sisters had been so proud when she came out, and she had such a send-off from Colinton, and she could not bear to come home having failed'. While feeling sorry for a woman whom they had put into post, and commenting that 'we must not hurt her in getting her out', Elsie was also exasperated by her: 'She isn't a bit proud of the Hospital or the work there. She said to one orderly, who was ill, "Don't you think you should send into Paris for a *man*"! Not joking remember!'

The quality of people appointed to key positions made all the difference to the success or failure of units. Royaumont was lucky, for the most important appointment of all, the Chief Medical Officer, Frances Ivens, proved a brilliant leader. In that same letter Elsie could tell Mrs Laurie: 'Dr Ivens' management of the place, and her patience and persistence in the face of really extraordinary difficulties in the way of red tape etc. has made our work there really something to be proud of.' And, indeed, the hospital remained active throughout the war, gaining enormous respect, and many official honours, for the fine work of all the women there.

The April visit to Royaumont was in fact carried out en route to Serbia. A second SWH unit had travelled there in December. The country was being extolled for its determination and 'pluck' in fighting off the Austrians, but after the invasion came wounds and diseases — especially typhus — so the need for medical assistance was acute. The unit was sent to Kraguievac, a military key point near Belgrade. Their personnel was geared to a 100-bed hospital; instead they were given 250 beds, but with Austrian prisoners to help as additional orderlies. The horrendous typhus epidemic did not confine itself to soldiers or Serbs: between the time of their arrival in January, and March, two nurses and an woman orderly died of the disease.

During those months Elsie was torn between her desire to oversee the fund-raising and organisational work in Britain and her desire to serve in the field. In mid-April came a telegram saying that the Chief Medical Officer, Dr Eleanor Soltau, was ill with diphtheria. There is no mention anywhere of an attempt to find anyone else as a replacement; Elsie clearly saw this as divine providence. 'So the question of whether or not I am to go out has been settled!', she wrote simply to the committee.

She took with her as 'probationary' administrator the Hon. Evelina Haverfield. Evelina had been an early supporter of the Pankhursts, but after they resorted to arson she started a new suffrage society. She wrote to Elsie offering to go to Serbia, paying all her own expenses. Elsie on meeting her liked her very much and 'thought it would be a good opportunity of finding out exactly what she is worth, so I took her, on the distinct understanding that the Committee have not engaged her, that she absolutely obeys orders, and that we are not committed to keep her until I see what the work is like and if she would be useful. She speaks a great many languages, and has been very useful so far.'

In early May they arrived in Kraguievac where the unit was running three separate hospitals: one surgical, one typhus, and one 'Relapsing Fever' and general disease. The surgical hospital was a schoolhouse in the town, which held 170 beds, mostly full. The wards were small, 'and there are too many beds in each according to our standards, but much fewer than there are in other Hospitals I have seen here.' Dr Lilian Chesney, in charge, was 'doing excellent work.' The typhus hospital was a barracks on the outskirts of the town. It too was 'over-crowded from our standard, but is clean, and fresh and well arranged.' The third hospital was right out of town, 'had no equipment to speak of', and was being worked by only one doctor under the director and one Sister. 'This, of course, sounds ridiculous,' wrote Elsie to the committee, 'and it is so in a sense. There is not any real nursing, or proper doctoring. But there is no denying that these two women have worked wonders in the place. The Austrian orderlies are kept up to their duties. The patients at any rate get the medicines which are ordered for them, and the place is fairly clean.' In Elsie's opinion the unit 'were both understaffed and underequipped' for their work — 'they made themselves responsible for something like 570 beds!' However, she could well understand 'how they were almost driven into it, in the face of the awful need of the Country, and there is no doubt at all that they have done it excellently, and with a wonderful self-devotion.'

She considered, however, that there was a 'great want of discipline in the Unit.' She felt that Dr Soltau's hand 'was not strong enough for the very difficult team she had to drive', and, at the same time, instead of receiving the support she should have had from the other doctors she 'met with only barren criticism.'

Elsie also thought that the matron had not sufficiently looked after the comforts of unit members. Various changes were therefore made by

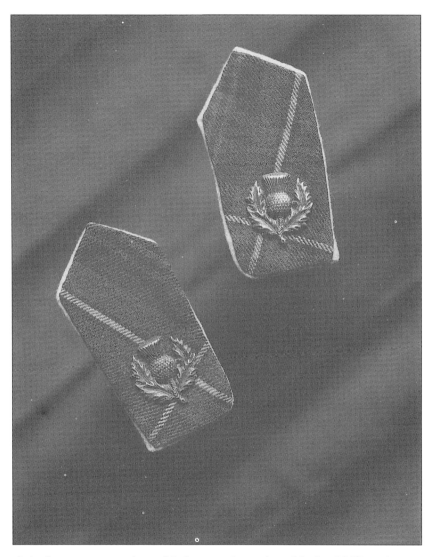

Pair of tartan gorget patches and badges worn by members of the Scottish Women's Hospitals.

Elsie, but she was able to report to the committee that 'the work that has been done is beyond praise'.

By now funds had been raised to equip two further units, one of which went to Troyes in France and subsequently joined the French Expeditionary Force in Salonica, where it served for the duration of the war under the fine leadership of Dr Louise McIlroy. Another Serbian unit, under Dr Alice Hutchison, was briefly detained in Malta after the debacle of the Dardanelles (the only occasion on which an SWH unit was able to treat British and Commonwealth soldiers), before continuing to Serbia.

When Elsie arrived there in early May the typhus epidemic was still out of control, though relief was coming in many forms. A new scheme was to form a quarantine and disinfecting station at Mladenovac, the main railway junction used by soldiers on leave. Colonel William Hunter, head of an RAMC advisory mission, urged Elsie to undertake this. Subsequently it was decided to form three such SWH hospitals in different spots. The drive to Mladenovac was Elsie's first experience of Serbian roads, which involved at least fifty skids and constant 'bumping'. At one point they 'charged a string of boulders, which had been used to mend the road, and *got over them*; but it was the most glorious run as regards scenery. For a long way the road ran along the top of hills and valleys, and the lights and shadows were magnificent. I don't know when I enjoyed anything so much.'

Evelina Haverfield had proven to be a fine worker, and Elsie was very pleased when the committee ratified her appointment as administrator. On 22 June she described 'such a funny scene' that had occurred the day before. Water was much needed ('an English Hospital — taking English in a broad sense, needs a lot more water than a Serbian one!)' — and that morning none had arrived. Evelina was told that one watercart was broken, and no one knew where the second one was. She came to Elsie very angry, when 'suddenly we saw a water-cart stravaighing quietly along the road. Without one word she ran like a hare... seized the horse by its bridle, and marched it off to the Barrels, while the driver crouched on the top (even across the camp you could see how helpless and scared he was) still holding the reins.'

The establishment of the Mladenovac hospital under Dr Beatrice Macgregor, an old colleague from the Bruntsfield, helped to solve a clash of personalities. Both Evelina Haverfield and Dr Lilian Chesney were highly temperamental and took strong likes and dislikes to people; their mutual antipathy was strong, and it was therefore helpful to be able to send Evelina to Mladenovac.

Elsie was truly happy that summer. She was doing general surgery on grown men, which had been almost impossible for a woman before the war, and had won the respect of Serbian medical men. She was consulted by men like Colonel Hunter and had scope for her administrative talents. And she had fallen in love with the Serbs *en masse*. It was not an uncritical love — she faced bureaucracy, obfuscation, and mysterious delays right from the start — but it went deep. Already she was planning not only for the present but for improved medical services in Serbia after the war. In a letter home she wrote that the Serbs were 'a very charming people, very like the Irish, in almost every way, but much better looking.'

Colonel Hunter was ordered to Malta in June. After Elsie Inglis' death he wrote about her in *The Times*: 'I have never met with anyone who gave me so deep an impression of single-mindedness, gentle-heartedness, clear and purposeful vision, wise judgement, and absolutely fearless disposition'.

In July the heads of British units in Serbia met to consider their role in a country where there was no fighting and no longer much disease. Elsie felt strongly that 'we should wait here in readiness for emergencies which must come', for when those emergencies did come 'there will be no country in more need than Serbia — with under 300 doctors and no nurses whatever.' The general feeling, she reported back to the committee, was that 'dull or not dull, it is our duty to stick to our posts', and at the end of the conference a resolution was passed that no British unit should leave Serbia.

One problem when work was slack was to maintain 'discipline' amongst high-spirited, 'emancipated' young women in a country of charming, handsome men. 'If you hear that the Scottish Sisters flirt, *say they don't*', she wrote to the committee, 'and next time I can send a letter home by hand, I'll explain.' Later she wrote that 'Our naughtiest girls were some of those who had worked right through the typhus without funking or grumbling'. She came down on them with a heavy hand, for she felt a strong sense of responsibility for her 'girls' and for maintaining the reputation of the SWH. She was also, of course, a Victorian by upbringing, so that strict, even prudish, standards, were part of her character.

But there were plenty of harmless diversions laid on, like picnics and theatricals. Dr Chesney arranged a successful 'sports day' for staff and patients, including an egg-and-spoon race and a crutch race. Elsie was struck by the way 'we all were — Turks and British and Serbs and Austrians, all playing together as happy as possible. Perhaps if we played more together, and knew one another better, such awful things as this war would not happen.'

Her latest scheme was to take over an existing Serbian hospital at Lazarevac, putting Dr Edith Hollway, who liked the Serbs very much, in charge. Her idea was to use equipment made on the spot by local craftsmen, rather than imported from Britain, to show the Serbs what could be done in their own traditional ways, and also to reveal to them any shortcomings in those traditional methods. She later wrote: 'These beloved Serbians — you cannot help loving them, but they are the most awful people to work with. Dear old Col Grutich at one point wanted us to give up Lazarovatz because there were so many difficulties and he hated us to have difficulties! I told him *we loved them* — and the more difficulties there are the more spice there is in overcoming them.' The hospital was a success and also provided a suitable posting as administrator for Evelina Haverfield, who had by now fallen out with Dr Beatrice Macgregor at Mladenovac.

Sanitation was the main problem with every hospital in Serbia. Sewage normally drained through holes in the floor to a ditch under each ward, and from there to a pool in the central yard, covered with an ill-fitting wooden lid, uncleaned for years at a time. At Kraguievac Elsie organised the massive job of emptying the cesspit and creating 'a slope on which a cart for two barrels will stand, and all dirty water will be emptied into them and carted to the fields'. They had 'filled in the awful pit or pond', she advised, 'and the Serbians have tidied up the grass, which is so like them, the dear things. While we struggle with the cesspool they make the grass nice.' The importance of hygiene was emphasised at Dr Alice Hutchison's hospital, where, in spite of the most stringent efforts by her unit, three doctors and three nurses fell ill with enteric fever, and one of the nurses died.

As the summer wore on tension rose, for after the typhus epidemic was over there was little to stop the Germans and Austrians invading the country. But on 7 September there took place the ceremony of unveiling and benediction of a stone fountain bringing pure water to Mladenovac which had been built by the Serbs as a memorial to Dr Inglis. The party accompanying her left Kraguievac only an hour later than planned, 'quite good for this dear unpunctual country.' The ceremony was attended by men of all branches of the army, SWH unit members, and some local people. Five Orthodox priests in flowing robes chanted the service. Basil, dipped in holy water, was sprinkled over the fountain and over the soldiers, and, in a speech which Elsie could not understand as it was in Serbo-Croat, the country's gratitude to Dr Inglis was expressed. She knew that they weren't used to women speaking, so rather than try and respond with a speech in English or French she 'thanked them a thousand times and they did not seem to expect anything more.' She then turned on the flow of the fountain, and was presented with the basil sprigs.

Thus closed their 'long, peaceful summer' in Serbia. Autumn was upon them, and hostile forces were massed on the borders to engulf them all.

Elsie Inglis, 1916.

4

Serbia prided itself on being the only country so far to repel invasion, and the Serbs were convinced that the Allies would help them when the enemy again attacked. Serbia was a small but strategic nation, straddling the trans-European railway. Seizing Serbia would allow free movement of troops, armaments and supplies, and greatly strengthen the link between Germany and Turkey. Yet this obvious move seems to have escaped the Allied generals, obsessed as they were with the Western Front. The Bulgarians, seeing this, threw in their lot with the Germans, and a secret treaty was signed on 6 September 1915. Germans, Austrians and Bulgarians encircled Serbia with a force of over 400,000 men, an attack far more immense than anything envisaged by the Allies.

'If only', Elsie wrote to the committee on 26 September, 'they could have sent a British Expeditionary Force up here this summer, it would have made absolutely all the difference — all the Balkan States would have declared on our side, Germany could not have got ammunition through to the Turks, and probably things would have been easier for Russia. I suppose one ought not to criticise — but to lengthen our line in France and have muddling diplomacy out here!'. Later she wrote more forcefully to her sister about the 'idiots at the top who had not enough gumption to *know* this must happen. Anybody, even us women, could have told them that the Germans must try and break through to the help of the Turks.' Initiated by the French, an expeditionary force was sent out, but it was too little too late, and at the end of September, when the invasion began in earnest, it had to retreat to Salonica where it remained for the duration of the war.

'As long as the Serbians fight, we'll stick to them', Elsie wrote home. On 8 October Belgrade fell. Mladenovac was on the main railway line, so on the 12th Dr Beatrice Macgregor had to evacuate her unit. They set up an emergency dressing station at Kraguievac and were soon handling about 400 cases a day. The last hospital to be evacuated was Dr Hollway's at Lazarevac, because it lay behind the hills, and the Serbs had hoped to make a stand there. However, this unit too had to leave hurriedly. After a three-day journey of 100 miles they reached Krusevac where they were given a barracks outbuilding, known as Czar Lazar, in which to open a hospital. The surgical hospital at Kraguievac was full to overflowing, with beds increased from 125 to 175, and the SWH also took over two guesthouses, with an additional 140 beds.

Elsie hoped desperately that they would be able to remain there — it was, after, all the spot where the Serbian stand of 1914 had halted the enemy. Confusion reigned supreme in Serbia at that time, and neither the Scottish Women, nor any one else, knew what was happening. The retreat of the Allies back to Salonica after their abortive attempt to come to the aid of Serbia was not yet common knowledge, so until the last minute there was hope of succour. However, on 21 October the Germans got two bridges over the Danube, and Kraguievac, Serbian army headquarters, was their first objective. On the 23rd the unit received orders to leave, and, after pleading unsuccessfully that wounded men needing surgery were still arriving, Elsie arranged the clearing of the hospital, with every man who could possibly move being sent off by train, by bullock wagon, or even on foot.

By the afternoon of the 25th the hospital was almost cleared, but twenty cases were too serious to move. Two nurses volunteered to do final dressings, and Elsie stayed with them until the last moment. Heartbroken at abandoning patients for whom she was responsible, she vowed that it would never happen again.

Arriving in Krusevac Elsie was allocated a school building and, as she had brought all her equipment, soon had a functioning hospital. She was critical of Dr Hollway's Czar Lazar hospital; obviously conditions were difficult, but to tolerate overcrowding and poor hygiene was just not acceptable. However, soon after this came the crunch: there was no longer any hope of holding Serbia and only one escape route out of the country, over the Montenegrin and Albanian mountains to Scutari. The Allies persuaded the Serbs to retreat via that route and save what they could of their army to fight again another day. Individual members of the SWH now had the choice of joining in that retreat or remaining behind.

Neither option was an easy one. Those who joined the retreat experienced nightmare conditions, climaxing in a blizzard at the top of the pass. Over 100,000 soldiers and civilians died in that retreat, and amongst the dead was an SWH nurse whose cart was hurled over the edge of a mountain road.

Elsie and the others who remained behind with her (and with Alice Hutchison) faced a different kind of ordeal, but in her last letter to her committee (carried by those on the retreat) she wrote that if they 'could have seen Colonel Gentitch's face when I said to him that we were not going to move again but that they could count on us just where we stood, I think you would have been touched.' The retreat party was delayed a day, so Elsie added a letter to her sister: 'We are in the very centre of the storm and it just feels exactly like having the rain pouring down, and the wind beating in gusts, and not being able to see for the water in one's eyes and just holding on and saying "It cannot last, it is so bad". These poor little people, you cannot imagine anything more miserable than they are'. She wondered 'if Serbia is a particularly beautiful country, or whether it looks so lovely because of the tragedy of this war, just as bed seems particularly delightful when the night bell goes!'

On 6 November the women who had elected to stay felt a sense of anticlimax until, in the late afternoon, a great explosion blew out most of the windows in the hospital and of the house where the unit was quartered. An ammunitions train had been blown up by the Serbs to destroy a railway bridge. In response there was an enemy bombardment. The unit slept that night on the floor of their damaged hospital and moved into new quarters the next day, by which time the Germans had arrived. At first Elsie was favourably impressed. They were courteous and disciplined and praised her hospital. The next day they asked her if she would look after German wounded, and she agreed. But then they demanded that all her Serb patients be removed to the prefecture, and then, the day after that, demanded that they be moved again, this time to the Czar Lazar Barrack

Hospital. The double move was quite unnecessary, and because the Germans were so efficient Elsie was convinced this ill treatment must have been deliberate. And then — the final blow — she and her nurses were also forced to leave the hospital she had created and go to work at the Czar Lazar. When she protested to the Serbian hospital director, Major Nicolitch, he said that 'of course' the Germans had taken her hospital; 'You had made it so beautiful.'

From then on both her unit and that of Dr Hollway worked at the Czar Lazar, which became an official prisoner-of-war hospital (her unit was in the main building and Dr Hollway's in the 'magazine'). They lived in as well. 'You can imagine that we have plenty to do,' she wrote to her sister on 30 November, 'when you hear we have 900 wounded. The prisoners are brought every day, sometimes thousands, and go on to the north, leaving the sick.' Subsequently numbers rose to 1,200. The two buildings were meant to accommodate 400 fit soldiers, but this was the only hospital in the town for the Serbs, so Elsie was forced to overcome her scruples about overcrowding.

The unit was also made responsible for sanitation, and the hospital compound at that time was 'a truly terrible place — the sights and smells beyond description'. Their accomplishment (with a squad of prisoner orderlies) in cleaning and sanitising it, leaving it 'not, it is true, exactly like an English park, but at least clean', was, in Elsie's eyes the finest achievement of the Scottish Women while they were prisoners.

She was similarly gratified at the outcry when new wounded prisoners were put into the wards: 'if you put these dirty men in among us, we shall all get typhus', they wailed. At last, she thought, because of the SWH and other British hospital units, the Serbs had grasped the link between dirt and disease. Typhus was, in fact, her own greatest fear, for it was rife in the occupying army. She appealed to the authorities for more premises but was refused and finally opened a small building at the far end of the hospital grounds as a fever annexe. In the end she was able to report triumphantly that they had not had a single case of typhus.

It was bitterly cold. By the end of November they had already had a hard frost for several days, and blizzards. 'My warm things did not arrive', she advised her sister, 'Fortunately, last year's uniform was still in existence, and I wear three pairs of stockings, with my high boots. We have all cut our skirts short, for Serbian mud is awful.' However, there were compensations: 'It is a lovely land, and the views round here are very cheering. One sunset I shall never forget — a glorious sky, and the hills deep blue against it. In the foreground the camp fires, and the prisoners round them in the fading light.'

Food was in short supply. The unit lived mainly on black sour bread and bean soup, with a small amount of meat, and no milk or eggs. However, physical privation was easier to cope with than their total isolation. A band of women working in a Serbian prisoner-of-war hospital under German occupation, they had no way of knowing what was happening anywhere else, and wild rumours abounded.

On 24 November the Germans were preparing to depart from Krusevac (having secured the railway, they were leaving occupation duties to Austrians and Bulgarians), and before going they made a seemingly innocuous request of Dr Inglis, that she should sign a certificate attesting to the good behaviour of the German Army. She hesitated, discussed it with her colleagues, and decided to refuse. The troops had certainly behaved well enough while they were there, but to sign a statement of this bare fact while 'shut up in a small Serbian village and cut off from news of everything that was going on the rest of Serbia — and the rest of the world — might give an absolutely false impression.'

She conveyed her decision to the authorities. Back came an angry message: she must sign the certificate. Ah, then she was right, the request could not have been as innocent as it seemed. She would not sign. Of course it was of no importance, came the German response, but the High Command was angry and would issue an order; if she did not sign then the whole unit might be removed to Germany. 'If it is a matter of no importance', she said, 'I fail to understand why the High Command should know anything about the matter or why it should make them angry. But if it is an affair of sufficient importance to interest the High Command, I wish to know just why it is important, before I sign.' She was told nothing but was browbeaten and threatened. The certificate, when it was handed to her to sign, was in German, and when she protested that she would have first to understand what she was supposed to be signing, the commanding officer said, 'It is nothing; just to say you have been well treated and that you have nothing to complain of'. When she continued to refuse, the attitude of the commanding officer became more menacing, but she refused to be daunted, and in the end it was a stand-off, and she

Schweizer Illustrierte Zeitung *reports the arrival in Zurich of Elsie Inglis and other members of the Scottish Women's Hospitals after their release as prisoners of war, 1916.*

was allowed to return to the hospital. Later she told her sister how she felt at that time: 'It was a great day in my life when I discovered that I did not know what fear was.'

It was only when she arrived back in Britain that Elsie learned the significance of the request. Four weeks earlier Edith Cavell had been shot by the Germans as a spy and had immediately become a national heroine. The shock was still reverberating, with the Germans figuring as brutes and barbarians. A testament signed by Dr Elsie Inglis, well known in Britain (and even in uncommitted America), would have had great counter-propaganda value for the Germans.

The final weeks of 1915 were difficult. Food was scarce, there were miseries like dysentery, and permanently damp feet from that awful mud, and they had to watch the sufferings and demoralisation of the Serbian people. At the beginning of December Alice Hutchison briefly found herself there and later wrote: 'I had up till then felt that we in no way merited the title of "the heroic band of women". I came away from Dr Inglis's Hospital feeling that they *had* earned it. Picture over twenty people — including the head of the hospital — dining and sleeping and eating and washing in one room; picture all their equipment gone and them looking after Serbs in the best way they could in hospital corridors. They were, however, wearing no air of martyrdom.' And Elsie wrote of that time that her sorrow was 'shot through with a strange happiness'.

At the end of December many unit members took up an offer of repatriation (though in fact they were detained so long en route that it was February before they reached home). Elsie, Evelina Haverfield, and a few others were determined to stay in Serbia as long as possible. Patients continued to arrive, and by mid-January the hospital still had its optimum 400. Elsie and the others tried hard to keep their hopes up about some kind of Allied breakthrough, but in February they were notified that they must leave. Evelina Haverfield, and two others, concocted a scheme to conceal themselves in a nearby village so as to be left behind, but when the departure date was changed their absence was noticed, so they had to join the others. The group was kept in Vienna for a few days, then sent to Zurich, reaching home on 29 February.

Most of the repatriated women took a holiday, but not Elsie, who threw herself into fund-raising and new plans. The Scottish 'heroines', both those who had taken part in the trek across the mountains, and those who had remained behind enemy lines, were lionised by the press. After a meeting in Glasgow Elsie was written of as a 'bright-faced little woman in a grey uniform who spoke modestly, almost shyly, of her work among the Serbians and referred to the risks she had run as if they were everyday and commonplace'. The money poured in, and not only in Britain. Elsie had also been the first to recognise the potential of a young woman named Kathleen Burke who was working in the office. She had charm and charisma, and after she went to America to raise funds there she became known as the 'thousand dollar a day girl'. In the course of several tours of the United States and Canada she raised about a quarter of all SWH money. A new unit, known as the 'America' unit, went out to Macedonia and, after the armistice, followed the victorious troops to start a hospital in Serbia.

In April 1916 Elsie was decorated by the Crown Prince of Serbia with the Order of the White Eagle, the highest honour his country could bestow. Many Serbian refugees had ended up on the island of Corsica, and another SWH unit which had been destined for Serbia, went there to serve instead. Elsie visited the hospital later that month and was full of praise for the work being done.

However, Elsie still longed to serve her own countrymen. One obvious place to do so was Mesopotamia. It was not until the following year that the truly appalling standards of medical care there were made public, but Elsie had received an inkling from private sources and was determined to send an SWH unit there. The difficulty was that Mesopotamia was the responsibility of the Indian Government working directly under the War Office, and the War Office was as hostile to medical women as it had been in 1914. In summer 1915, capitalising on the praise given to the work of Alice Hutchison's unit at Malta, the SWH committee had offered the War Office a unit for service at Malta, Alexandria or elsewhere, but was flatly refused. Now, a year later, the lengths to which the War Office went to frustrate them were quite extraordinary.

Dr Inglis went to see Captain Padham who was in charge of all the arrangements for Mesopotamia, and he took her to see General Russell. Both officers told her that the Indian Government applied to their department for whatever was needed; it was not the business of the department to *offer* the Indian Government anything. From this she understood that the offer of a hospital must be made to the Viceroy. An official telegram was sent offering the Indian Government a fully staffed and equipped hospital of 200 beds for service in Mesopotamia. In addition Lady Cowdray, of the London committee, who knew the Viceroy personally, sent him a separate telegram, and received a reply stating that the offer was much appreciated, but that the offer should be referred to the War Office.

Elsie was visiting the unit in Corsica at that time, but as soon as she returned she took the telegram to Captain Padham. Ah but, he said, it did not actually ask for a hospital; it left the War Office to decide, which it would if it was asked, but it had not been. So off went another telegram to the Viceroy saying that the Indian Government should apply to the War Office for the hospital. In the meantime the committee received a letter from the Viceroy stating that the offer had been accepted, that it was a 'splendid one and will, I am sure, be of the greatest service to the army in Mesopotamia.' When the Viceroy advised the War Office of this good news, he was cabled, 'Can send you all the hospitals you may require you should not accept others as long as we can supply'.

Elsie returned to Captain Padham, clutching a growing pile of correspondence. The Captain claimed that this was the first he had heard of the offer, acceptance, and War Office telegram, but he thought 'that by now the Indian Government had got all the hospitals they needed.' However, he took Dr Inglis to General Russell again, and the latter admitted that the Indian Government had asked for the Scottish Women's Hospital. He could give no reason for the refusal 'except that as long as the War Office had hospitals of their own they should use them.' He suggested that Dr Inglis should put the whole case in writing and send it to the Secretary of the War Office.

This was done, but subsequently, when she went to see him he 'absolutely and definitely refused a hospital for Mesopotamia on the ground that there were already plenty of Hospitals there, and adequate help of every kind.' That was an out-and-out lie, and Elsie wanted to raise hell, but the committee backed off, perhaps recoiling from such an unpleasant conflict or possibly feeling simply that the time and effort needed for this were better utilised in other ways. Lady Cowdray suggested that the SWH immediately send a representative to India 'to find out the position as to hospitals there, with the hope that should a real need exist, a Scottish Women's Hospital unit might be taken under the Indian

Government.' She also suggested that 'the representative should also conduct a campaign for raising money at the same time.' Elsie's sister, Eva Shaw McLaren, had in fact been out in India and started a fund-raising campaign there but advised that it needed 'someone who can give their whole time. The distances are tremendous.'

Elsie, of course, had been brought up in India, and the committee wanted her to go (possibly as much to divert her from her proposed campaign against the Government over Mesopotamia as for any other reason), but she was not keen to be so far from the centre of action and therefore refused. She suggested Elizabeth Abbott, a member of the executive committee of the NUWSS who at one time had been employed as an organiser for the Edinburgh National Society for Women's Suffrage. Mrs Abbott agreed and set off in June.

At that time two Serbian divisions were being recruited in southern Russia from Austrian Slavs who had deserted to the Allies; unable to return to Serbia, they were eager to volunteer to fight with the Russians. In response to a request from the Serbian Government, Elsie asked the committee if they would 'be willing to supply a Hospital for this force.' On 9 June the committee 'resolved that this request be granted, provided that Dr Inglis will herself take out the Unit.' Those seemingly innocuous words lit a short fuse under Elsie, who had been harbouring a host of grievances and now exploded. 'Sorry cannot take any more Units out under Scottish Hospitals', she telegraphed from London where she was fund-raising, 'Desire also to resign commissionership'.

This was a bombshell. Where would the Scottish Women's Hospitals be without Elsie, and what had driven her to this step?

5

When, back in 1909, Elsie suddenly decided to sever links with the Bruntsfield Hospital, the repercussions for the work there did not, apparently, cross her mind; she had decided to go, and that was that. Her rift with the Scottish Women's Hospitals followed a similar pattern.

What galled Elsie was the committee's mentality: 'Apparently it is not a question of "Is the Unit needed", only of who will take it. The Unit may be needed, but if I don't take it, it is not to go.' This she saw as symptomatic of a fundamental difference over 'the ideal the Scottish Women's Hospitals should have before them in this war'. One committee member had 'put the question in a nutshell. "We have done so well that now, I think, we ought to consolidate what we have done. You think that because you are ambitious for the Women's Question that we should launch out and do more." Without arguing the question of my motives, that is exactly the point. Because the Scottish Women's Hospitals have played such a wonderful role in the war — have relieved so much suffering and helped so much — we ought to go on... Why should we stop to "consolidate" just when the need of help is greatest? With our past history and our magnificent backing it appears to me our duty to push forward.'

After meeting with the committee Elsie held to her resignation as commissioner — and added her resignation as a committee member, and therefore as honorary secretary. 'It was quite clear at the end of our talk that there is a very great divergence between me and the Committee, and all the kind things that we said could not magic away "the gulf".' However, as the committee 'seemed to be quite unanimous in feeling that my total separation from the Hospitals would injure the work, carried on even on their lines', she agreed to take out the new Serbian unit.

Another of the committee's decisions at this time emphasised the contrast in approach. Evelina Haverfield had offered to take out a transport column (one such SWH column was already operating in Macedonia), along with Dr Inglis' unit. The committee asked her 'to take charge of the cars in Dr Inglis' Unit, as the Committee did not feel justified in undertaking any additional new schemes at present.' This was awful. Elsie wrote to Mrs Laurie, the treasurer (the only committee member with whom she felt in sympathy): 'What I thought was decided was that the transport given to me should be formed into a Field Ambulance *attached to my Hospital*. In this way they would be always available to transport my Hospital, but could be used for all the Hospitals in the division — And you should not think it is a case of "What's in a name?". There is everything in the name — "The Flying Field Ambulance attached to Scottish Women's Hospital Unit No.2" is a *thing*. "*My cars*" are nothing... dear Mrs Laurie, do make people realize that all the spirit is taken out of people if they are checked instead of encouraged. You cannot expect Mrs H. to be as interested in "looking after my cars" as in her own Field Ambulance. There is such a thing as making people proud of their job, and interested in its success'.

All this was very reasonable, as were her comments in a subsequent letter: 'Nobody could be more sorry than me to resign. But it was no good pretending that the Committee as a whole really shared my aspirations or approved of my methods. And the result was that we formed a disastrous explosive mixture that might have wrecked the Hospitals! So I removed myself — for the common good.'

The trouble was that Elsie did not in fact 'remove' herself until the unit departed at the end of August, and in the meantime Elizabeth Abbott had reached India and was writing back to her with an account of the tricky negotiations she was engaged in for an SWH unit in Mesopotamia. A 'paddle boat, 50 beds, fans, etc. accompanied by Nurses and Doctors to ply between Kut and Basra would be a good thing', she wrote, and the Commander in Chief told her she might quote him to all the officials it was necessary to see, including the Viceroy, 'as supporting the acceptance of any good offer from us.' (Elizabeth had given him an account of the SWH's negotiations with the War Office, 'at which he was perfectly scandalised'.) The committee sent her a telegram advising her that since her departure they had taken on new responsibilities and could not supply a unit for Mesopotamia, so that she should confine her efforts to collecting money for general funds.

But then the committee had a letter from Elsie, 'indicating the lines on which she had instructed Mrs Abbott concerning her work in India.' As these instructions 'included a definite offer of a Hospital from the SWH Committee, either for Mesopotamia or Karachi or Bombay, the Committee felt that they could not agree with Dr Inglis, that these were their instructions.' Poor Elizabeth Abbott was caught in the middle, being advised by Elsie, who had recruited her for the work, to go ahead with negotiations — as late as September Elsie was still writing to her that 'rather than have the Scottish Women's Hospitals put in an invidious position, the offer of a ship should hold good' — and by the committee to concentrate solely on fundraising (their letter to her reiterated 'the Committee's decision that neither a ship nor anything else can be given, and that Dr Elsie Inglis no longer voices the wishes of the Committee').

Another bone of contention was the role of the London Committee. Elsie felt that there was a great deal that could only be done from London, but the Edinburgh-based committee were jealous of their own authority and determined that London would not usurp any of it. Elsie was in the centre of the wrangle — it was decided that her unit, and Evelina Haverfield's transport column, were to go out under the aegis of the London Committee, though Headquarters Committee in Edinburgh would pay salaries — and the Edinburgh chairman, Mrs Hunter, thought that Elsie's 'conduct to us has been simply disgraceful and in my opinion she is doing all she can to cause a split between us and London. She is apparently guided by a vindictive, unjust spirit and not by a sense of right and wrong.'

Such a judgment is at odds with everything that is known of Elsie Inglis and is not echoed anywhere else, though there is no doubt that Elsie was better at 'gingering' than at conciliating. At this particular time, having fallen out so badly with the Edinburgh committee, she clearly 'bonded' with the group in London, with whom she remained on the very best of terms.

Her unit, and Mrs Haverfield's transport column (a total of 75 women) left Liverpool on 29 August 1916. 'Dr Inglis likes a great deal of deference paid to her as head of the unit', a medical student, Ellie Rendel, wrote to her mother, 'and she goes in for roll calls, cabin inspection etc.' The second half of the statement was certainly true, for Elsie reported to the London committee: 'We have breakfast at 8.30, and after that Cabins are tidied. Roll-call is at 9.30 and immediately after is Cabin Inspection. At 10 o'clock there is drill... Drill is compulsory. Lunch is at 12.30, and during the afternoon are classes in Russian, Serbian and French, and also classes on motor construction, etc. None of these classes are compulsory, but almost all the Unit take one or the other. Tea is at 4 o'clock, and dinner at 6.30.'

'We have to stand to attention etc', wrote Ellie Rendel, 'and at roll call she has given the order that we are to say "Here Ma'am".' One morning Elsie announced that it was ridiculous to address women officers as 'Sir', so that they should instead be addressed, like royalty, as 'Ma'am'. Members of the transport thought this was absurd, so next morning each replied with some variant, everything from 'Madam' to 'Moddam' and 'Mum'. Everyone was convulsed with laughter — even Evelina Haverfield — everyone, that is, except Elsie, who 'maintained a rigid control and a look of strong disapproval' (one orderly thought that was 'her Scotch extraction for once predominating').

The ship docked at Archangel on 10 September. The unit was fêted, but the news from the front was dreadful. The Serbs, fighting alongside the Russians in Rumania had suffered appalling losses, with only 4,000 survivors out of 14,000 men. Elsie telegraphed home for vast extra quantities of ether, chloroform and dressings, and did everything she could to expedite the journey to Odessa. In spite of Elsie haranguing the railway staff, it took an interminable nine days.

Ellie Rendel wrote to her cousin at this time: 'Dr Inglis is not a good leader. She gets very much fussed and loses her temper easily, rapidly and often unjustly because she is in too great a hurry. Also she is very shy and can't make conversation. She takes no personal interest in anyone and is therefore not at all popular.' That last remark is belied by letters from orderlies at the same time, for example the one who commented: 'I *do* think Dr Inglis is simply splendid'. But the unit's cook, Mary Milne, was disappointed at the way 'the heads lose their tempers'. There was no suggestion of this happening in Serbia the year before, but Elsie was now under an enormous amount of stress.

There were about a thousand wounded soldiers in Odessa, and it was suggested that the unit remain there to take charge of them, with the motor transport being sent on to the front. Elsie told the General that she 'was ready to do whatever he wished, but I pointed out that if our transport left us we would become practically a stationary hospital and that we were not equipped for this. I therefore suggested that the British Red Cross Unit which was close behind us should be kept for this work… and that as field hospitals are immediately necessary with the First Division we should go on.' Even the hyper-critical Ellie Rendel had to admire this achievement: 'In some ways Dr Inglis is a very wonderful woman. She has got her own way in spite of many difficulties and has succeeded in making the unit a field hospital. The people in Odessa did their best to make her stay there. But she refused and insisted on being sent on. The Red Cross party who arrive later are going to be kept there instead. I expect Mr Berry [in charge of the Red Cross unit] will be furious'.

On 24 September they left for Medjidia, the Russian headquarters in the Dobrudja district of Rumania. The train journey to Reni on the Danube, where they would transfer to boats, normally took six hours; Elsie was warned that it would probably take twenty-four hours in wartime. In fact it took them three days and four nights. When they arrived she was given a barrack in which to form a base hospital; she would have preferred to move forward and open a field hospital, but the commanding officer would not consider it. 'The ordinary male disbelief in our capacity cannot be argued away. It can only be worked away', she wrote later.

Two days after their arrival the wounded came pouring in, and the pressure was intense. Ellie Rendel paints a picture of Elsie Inglis at this time which is again at odds with everything else that has been written about her: 'She flies into blind rages over trifles and is quickly reducing all her sisters [nurses] to tears.' Ellie gave one example: 'It was 10.30 p.m. and Dr I. was romping about trying to pierce a hole in a man's skull. She asked the sister for a certain instrument — a very common one without which no operation at home would be done. The sister said there wasn't one. Dr I. turned livid with rage and for 30 minutes abused the poor woman until she dropped glasses and smashed everything she touched and the tears rolled down her cheeks. Next morning Dr I. came along and examined the instruments for herself. She had to admit it wasn't there.' Ellie concluded: 'This incident is typical of Dr I. It ought to have been there. Dr I. ought to have examined all her instruments before leaving London and she ought not to fly into unreasonable passions.'

Was such behaviour really 'typical' of Elsie Inglis? It is highly improbable that she would have gained such a high reputation if this were true. Ellie Rendel was Lilian Chesney's protegée and hyper-critical of everyone, so she may have embellished a fairly minor incident. On the other hand, though she generously gave credit for good work, Elsie was intolerant of imperfection. However, the fact is that the commanding officer who had been so sceptical of this all-women's hospital was sufficiently impressed to request them to open a field dressing station nearer the front, and twelve members of her unit, under Dr Lilian Chesney, plus Evelina Haverfield's transport column, moved forward. (The antipathy between those two women was as great as ever, and their camps were side by side, which did not make for harmony.)

Elsie and her unit were at Medjidia for only three weeks, for the Germans were still advancing, the Russians and Rumanians still retreating, and the bombs falling. On 20 October she was ordered to evacuate the hospital and move back seventy-five miles to Galatz, but she continued to admit new patients. The next day the women began to pack the equipment. 'We did not finish until 4.30 in the morning', an orderly (L J Brown) wrote home, 'and all night long the sky was lit up by the flashes of the guns and the light of burning villages. We had orders to leave at 5.30 in the morning and at 11.30 Dr Inglis (our chief) was still considering the possibility of remaining! (She was taken prison in Serbia and loves it but some of us have views about being taken by the Bulgars!) Then she remembered it was Sunday — said that we would hold Divine Service at 2 o'clock P.M. (!) All the time the guns got nearer and along the road came a never ending stream of refugees and the whole army in retreat.'

But eventually that afternoon about half the unit, particularly those who had suffered from dysentery, were sent off by train. About an hour later the remainder departed — Elsie in the staff car driven by a member of the transport column, five in the ambulance, and seven perched on top of the equipment in a Russian lorry. Dr Chesney's group had already set off by a different route, as had Evelina Haverfield's transport column, and they ended up in different places.

Citation for Serbian cross of mercy, awarded to Miss M S Drummond.

Elsie's group spent their first night in a small cottage, sleeping on a trodden earth floor, though, after having been told that there was no food available, Elsie managed to procure bortsch, roast turkey, bread and tea. The next morning they saw once again the endless stream of refugees. To Elsie what seemed particularly pathetic was 'a piano perched on a cart, and on the cart in front of it a gorgeous red sofa, and the anxious little housewife. She must have taken such a pride in her little house and there it was all broken up around her.' Dr Inglis obtained a promise of transport for her women from Russian headquarters, a promise quickly forgotten. But then they met up with an Irish mercenary who had helped them before and who 'persuaded' a Russian lorry driver to take them to the nearest port on the Danube where they could get boats to Galatz.

Elsie, however, remained with her own two vehicles and a handful of women, and that evening they camped by the roadside, with Mary Milne, the cook, preparing them an impromptu meal. They brought cushions and rugs from the cars and sat around the fire, 'and a more delightful, merry meal could not be imagined'. The moment seemed to Elsie like 'a fairy tale', for, seen through the wood smoke were groups of soldiers, standing motionless, holding their horses, and marvelling at this group of women 'laughing and chatting, alone and within earshot of the guns'.

When they reached Ghersova the next day Elsie was asked set up a dressing station for the hundreds of wounded who were converging there. Sending on the cars and drivers she asked for three volunteers and for the next two days they tended the wounded, until the ambulances stopped arriving. Then they, too, boarded a steamer down the Danube.

Their goal was Galatz, the largest port in the area, but river traffic was blocked beyond Braila where they had to disembark. There turned out to be thousands of wounded men in Braila, with only one surgical hospital and one civilian hospital, and Dr Inglis was asked by the mayor if she could help. Her equipment had been sent on to Galatz, so surgical operations could not be performed, but at least they could do dressings. She had only one other doctor and one nurse with her that first night, but many of the transport women had been VADs and were pressed into service. The next morning she went round with the mayor to survey the town. The flood of wounded had been overwhelming, and 'there were still men lying about in empty houses with their uniforms on and the horrible smell of sepsis from their wounds', she reported. It was obvious that there was a need for another proper hospital, so Elsie ordered the equipment and unit members to come back from Galatz. By the end of October she had opened an operating theatre and wards, and the unit worked under high pressure for several weeks. 'The Unit as a whole has behaved splendidly, plucky and cheery through everything and game for any amount of work', she wrote to her sister.

In reality there had been more personality conflicts, mostly centring around Evelina Haverfield. There were also financial problems, for when the administrator, a kindly soul who had got on well with the girls, went home, Elsie 'was horrified to find, purely by accident, that the accounts had never once been balanced from the time we left home.' She would do her best until a new administrator came out, but she was well aware that she was not good at managing money, and confessed to the London committee that 'in addition to managing the unit and doing surgery, the prospect of doing what I loath, looking after money, nearly appals me!' She knew exactly the type of woman she needed as administrator: 'a gentlewoman tolerant of other people's views, good at managing money, and who can talk French well. Whoever comes *must be as strong as a horse.*'

Another discovery that horrified Elsie was that some members of the unit were *swearing*, which was 'disgusting and disagreeable' — worse, even, than *flirting*. The ringleaders were members of the transport, and though Elsie was 'quite sure that it was nothing but a stupid pose on the part of some of the girls', she had them up before her, 'and gave them the worst talking to they have ever had in their lives — and the rest of the Unit caught it for not having stamped it out'. One nurse put it to Dr Inglis that surely she liked outspoken girls? 'I told her I had never been so insulted in my life, that because I like the modern healthy out-of-door girl with her energy and resource and independence I should approve of language that I would not tolerate in a coster, was an impertinence.' Elsie was convinced that 'the whole feeling of the Unit is dead against it', but even Mary Milne, the cook, who was older than most, found the lecture 'quite absurd'. Partly it was a question again of protecting the reputation of the SWH, but arguably it also reflects the gulf between a Victorian feminist and the more liberated Edwardians.

The military strategy now was to stop the Germans along the Danube, with the Russians defending the bridges. As long as they held, the Dobrudja was still to be fought for, and the hospital at Braila would continue to find a useful role. However, toward the end of November German forces managed to cross the Danube, and, caught in a pincer, Bucharest fell on 6 December. Allies forces had to abandon the Dobrudja, and retreat to Reni and the lower Danube where the delta would form the new front line.

With Braila threatened, the hospital had to be evacuated, and the unit was ordered to move back to Galatz; it took them fifty-six hours to travel the fifteen miles. 'This has been our second retreat in less than three months,' Elsie reported to the London committee, 'and the Unit has behaved with its usual good temper and cheerfulness through this last, which I think has been the most uncomfortable retreat I have ever experienced: and I feel that I am becoming an old hand at them now.' But she was furious at Mary Milne, who had been travelling with another party looking after the equipment, because four sterilising drums had gone missing. As far as Elsie was concerned, looking after the equipment was a sacred duty, and when she learned of the loss — Mary recorded — she was 'simply savage — I never thought she could speak to me like that.'

Even Galatz was threatened, and one day the unit packed up to leave for Odessa, but in the end their orders were to remain. Elsie was 'very glad'. Their hospital was a slum building between the railway station and quay. There was plenty of accommodation but no light and (as usual) no drains. But Christmas Day was warm and springlike, and they had a party, singing carols and playing games. Two days later the hospital — the only one remaining in Galatz — was ready, and on the 30th the wounded arrived. Within the first couple of hours the hospital was full. At the beginning, by the light of oil lamps and candles, it was possible for Dr Inglis to examine each patient as he arrived, but the numbers of wounded arriving in the town — over a thousand a day for nearly a week — soon made this impossible. The most serious cases were sent to the Scottish Women's Hospital, the rest going on to Reni or Odessa. After her first twenty-four hours of supervising admissions and dressing wounds, Elsie spent the next day in the operating theatre.

Dr Inglis realised that she and her two colleagues could not possibly cope with the large numbers awaiting operations, but help was at hand. By a bizarre twist of war, a division of British Navy armoured cars was rattling round the Eastern Front under the command of Oliver Locker

Elsie Inglis, left, riding astride for the first time, at Reni in May 1917.

Lampson, and they had assisted the Scottish Women on previous occasions during the retreat. Now, like jokers in the pack, they turned up again in Galatz. A member of the squadron, Surgeon-Lieutenant Maitland Scott, offered his assistance, which in such an emergency Elsie gladly accepted, so Dr Scott and four male orderlies worked with the unit. The two surgeons operated for thirty-six hours with only a brief rest, while the other doctors and nurses looked after the ward patients and walking wounded. 'It was a terrible experience', Elsie later wrote to the London committee, 'Every single case a bad one — poor, poor fellows'.

On 3 January the hospital was under control and work was slackening, but only because the opposite bank of the Danube was already in the hands of the Germans, and resistance to the enemy was coming to an end. On the 4th the order was given to evacuate. Commander Gregory, of the armoured car division, helped the main party of Scottish Women to safety, but Elsie and four others insisted on remaining with the patients until the last possible moment. In the almost deserted port there was little they could do for the wounded and dying, but to Commander Gregory, observing them soothing and comforting the men was 'a devotion to duty that was an example to us all'. Only after they were all seen off in Russian ambulances was Elsie prepared to leave, though once again she had left it dangerously late and seemed to be stranded. Then, out of nowhere, a naval barge appeared on the Danube and plucked her away to Reni. After this third retreat she wrote, 'Surely the luck will change now.'

6

The town of Reni in Rumania, where Elsie Inglis spent the next eight months, was small, and in peacetime it was insignificant. But it stood on the confluence of the River Pruth with the Danube, and on the main railway line to Odessa, so it became strategically important. When the unit arrived in early January 1917 there was no certainty that Reni could be held: 'Our own guns were firing from the hill above us and we saw Galatz on fire', reported Elsie to the London committee. And there were organisational problems to be sorted out, like who they were working for, and where they would get food, fuel and water. Fortunately, after a few days of chaos the head of the Russian Red Cross arranged for Dr Inglis to receive all the patients too badly wounded to move on in ambulance trains. He proved to be very helpful and efficient, and they were given an excellent building which had actually been designed as a hospital and was clean. The women's private quarters were also attractive, on high ground near the hospital with views over the Danube and hills beyond.

Elsie was somewhat flabbergasted when, on the day they had promised to have the hospital ready, 'when everybody was hard at it putting things into shape, and the wood and water problem was only being temporarily solved by the kindness of individual officers who lent us water-carts and gave us wood, two officers of the 30th Cossaks arrived on the scene with an invitation to a *concert*! And the "premier line" 7 versts off, and the guns booming all the time!' She accepted 'conditionally on there being no wounded', and in the evening the majority of the unit went off to the concert, 'which ended in a dance, and they got back at 1 a.m. just as the first batch of wounded arrived.'

For the first few days they were very busy indeed; then matters settled down to a reasonable routine. On 19 January the unit awoke to thick snow and ice, and a biting wind. This was the beginning of an exceptionally cold winter, which lasted until mid-March and even halted fighting on the Eastern Front. One day the house was cut off from the hospital by enormous snow drifts. Elsie wished she could have sent home a photograph 'of the Staff struggling over to Roll Call in the morning in their top boots, short skirts, and peaked *barliks* over their heads. The Danube has been frozen over, and the carts for wood crossed over on the ice. That is another photograph I wished I could have got: streams of men carrying wood across the river.'

Once the hospital was running smoothly Elsie travelled to Odessa to try and sort out two matters. The first was a mutiny by the transport column. They had done magnificent work during the retreats, but Evelina Haverfield's leadership qualities were called into question. The cars were out of commission at that point in any case, but the question of the future of the column still needed resolving. Dr Lilian Chesney's subordinate unit was at that time based in Odessa, and the personality clash between the two women had once again flared up. Elsie, admiring and able to get on with both of them, reported to London that 'they bring out the very worst in one another'. All she could suggest was that Evelina return home and report her side of the story to the London committee.

A more serious matter was the fact that the unit had come out to help the Serbs but had spent most of its time looking after the Russians. What was happening to the Serb divisions? From what Elsie gathered, they were in a difficult position. There was no love lost between them and the Russians, their numbers were greatly depleted, and they were unfit for battle.

The Russians really did need hospitals, and Serbian sick would be treated in those hospitals. When the Serbian Commander in Odessa told her that in the long term the Serbs would be better off if the Scottish Women's Hospitals went on working for the Russians rather than insisting on putting their hospitals under the Serbs (or — another possibility — go home until the Serbs needed them), Elsie accepted this. By the beginning of March she was able to report: 'We have got to like and admire our patients immensely.'

Dr Inglis opened a small out-patients' department, which enhanced their reputation. There was no difficulty in keeping the unit occupied even when work was slack, for 'every regiment which comes entertains us in some way.' The 'entertainments were most varied, — from a regimental concert in a dug-out, to a very smart concert and dance which the Black Sea Horse gave. (Isn't the Black Sea Horse a delightful name?) The concert in the dugout was most interesting. One Company was entertaining the rest of the regiment. I had no idea the Russian soldier had so much fun in him.' But Elsie, who felt obliged to act as chaperone, found the socialising much more of a strain than the work and was thankful when Lent arrived.

And then, in March, came the Russian Revolution. At first it seemed to most observers an entirely positive thing: it was 'most interesting to see how everybody is on the side of the change', Elsie wrote to her sister. In Reni, at least, discipline and morale were maintained. On 20 March the commander, Prince Dolgourokoff, paid the unit a surprise visit and decorated some of the wounded patients and all of the unit members who had taken part in the Dobrudja retreat with the St George's Medal 'for bravery under fire'. The patients rejoiced at the honour to their 'little sisters from Scotland'.

Having come to realise how much the Russians' religion meant to them, Elsie arranged for the purchase of four icons. They were placed in the corners of the wards, with tiny lamps burning always before them, and an army priest came to sprinkle holy water and bless them. She assured the committee back home that it was money justifiably spent, 'for it is a great thing in a foreign country to show the people that one has sympathy for them.'

However, all was not sweetness and light on the Eastern Front. The revolution had destabilised the situation, and the enemy was taking advantage. Spy fever raged, and, unbeknown to the Scottish Women, the authorities had been watching their house on the hill for some time and witnessed lights from the turret windows. On the night of 10 April soldiers came barging in to arrest the girl who slept up there. Sentries were placed round the house, and the orderly was given only enough time to put clothes on over her pyjamas before being marched to the office of the commander of the expeditionary force. Elsie insisted on going with her. She expected that they would simply have to answer a few questions, and the matter would be cleared up, but in fact they were locked up and refused permission to contact the British Consul or General Kropensky. After twelve hours they were still under confinement, and no one knew where.

It was the unit's enterprising matron who discovered their whereabouts and contacted an old friend, the admiral who commanded the Danube Russian Flotilla at Reni. Even he had to be careful in the new, unstable Russia, but he suggested that the whole unit sign a guarantee of the orderly's 'fidelity', which greatly angered them. After this was done and the women freed, a furious General Kropensky arrived and secured an apology from the colonel of the offending regiment, though after the General left another orderly, taking a walk and carrying two books, was arrested under the same suspicion. 'As you can imagine, this last incident simply added fuel to the dying flames of our wrath and the whole thing blazed up again', Elsie wrote to the London committee. They were tempted to withdraw their services, but, thinking it over, Elsie 'realised that we might do a great deal of harm by simply throwing up our work and going away leaving so false an impression of British subjects behind us... in common fairness we must look at the other side — a country in revolution with all the disorganisation which must inevitably accompany so great a change, even if that change be beneficial. The undoubted presence of spies all along the Front and the fact that foreigners by the ordinary people in any country are always regarded with suspicion'.

Easter celebrations in mid-April lightened the atmosphere. There was singing and dancing and cakes; and the men presented Elsie with a beautiful letter, which, in translation, began: 'We, all the patients, sick and wounded, belonging to the Army and Navy and coming from different parts of the Great Free Russia, who are at present in your hospital, are filled with feelings of the truest respect for you. We think it our duty as Citizens on this beautiful day of Holy Easter to express to you, highly respected and much beloved Doctor, as to your whole Unit, our best thanks for all the care and attention you have bestowed upon us.'

Russia that spring was wracked by mutinies, paranoia, and turmoil, but the flowers were glorious, and the unit was happy. Riding was their newest recreation, and Elsie overcame her Victorian upbringing to ride astride for the first time. And in early May the previous administrator (so hopeless with money, but such a familiar face) arrived with a large consignment of equipment, letters and all the latest news.

However, both she and the head of the transport section were so worried about the situation in Russia that they did not want to have any more women drivers. 'We should never have had any Scottish Women's Hospitals at all if they and their sort, dear things, had been listened to', wrote Elsie to the London committee, 'How they would have disapproved of Florence Nightingale's little band!'. As far as Elsie was concerned, 'the first object of the Scottish Women's Hospitals was to care for the wounded, and the second object was to do it through a womans organization, managed and officered by women'. Most humiliating was the fact that the Consul — 'without even seeing me' — had wired to the committee 'that it would be "criminal" to send out women!'. Such a thing would have been inconceivable 'if a man had been head of these hospitals'.

After talking with the transport head, Elsie reported to the committee that she had 'quite come back to her bearings'. However, the Foreign Office was so adamantly opposed to any women at all travelling out to such a trouble spot that in the end she had to accept a compromise: medical replacements could come out, but not women drivers.

At least — Elsie learned from a telegram in June — all those years of campaigning for the franchise, and working during the war, had achieved the goal: a Bill granting the vote to women over thirty had passed its second reading in the House of Commons. She thought it ironic that it had apparently taken a war to prove the importance of women's work: 'Where do they think the world would have been without women's work all these ages?'

But Elsie's main preoccupation during that summer of 1917 was the fate of the Serbian division. The Russian army was falling apart; if the Serbs had to fight alongside them on the Rumanian front none would survive. At one stage it appeared they were going to be sent to Salonica, but then that order was countermanded, and it seemed they would have to be sacrificed after all. Telegrams, letters, personal messages — Dr Inglis bombarded the British Prime Minister and Foreign Secretary with personal pleas to intervene.

Meanwhile, in August, the hospital in Reni was suddenly very busy again. An unsuccessful Russian offensive had been launched, and the most seriously wounded were sent to Dr Inglis' hospital. The hospital had been prepared to take 200 patients, but by 20 August there were 230. By then the trained nurses had left, and the new arrivals lacked surgical experience. The service was held together by orderlies, who were 'worth their weight in gold'. 'They have done splendidly', she advised London, 'and their training in military hospitals has stood them in good stead.'

A lighter moment came when a birthday telegram arrived from her sisters, to her delight and the bafflement of her administrator faced with a telegram printed in Cyrillics. 'She evidently was not used to people doing such mad things as telegraphing "Many happy returns of the day" half across the world. I understood it at once, and it nearly made me cry.'

On 31 August the unit left Reni and rejoined the Serb division in the village of Hadji Abdul in Bessarabia, formerly part of the Turkish empire, now filled with Rumanian refugees. For the first time the hospital and accommodation were under tents. They were dealing with sick and long-term wounded, so they were not under acute pressure but felt they were doing useful work. 'We have been very happy here', Elsie reported to the London committee in October, 'and have been most hospitably and kindly treated by the Serbs.'

Elsie's campaign to save the division — some 13,000 men — from annihilation on the Rumanian front had continued. Apart from writing letters to the authorities, she sent two of her most trustworthy orderlies home with a 2,500-word memorised message (only the headings were written down, on a piece of paper the size of a postage stamp), explaining the complexities of the situation. When asked to come home, she made it clear that she would not leave unless the Serbs were also sent to safety.

What no one at home had the slightest inkling of was that Elsie Inglis was mortally ill. Before setting off at the end of August 1916 she told her sisters that she had cancer, but she told no one else since she had made up her mind that she was going to survive. Because the very word 'cancer' was considered somehow shameful and therefore not to be mentioned, let alone discussed, there is no record of the type of cancer Elsie Inglis had, or precisely how it was affecting her. There are hints in earlier biographies of Elsie being 'unwell' as early as 1913 but no mention of her having undergone any surgery, so it must remain a mystery. Photographs of her taken in 1917 are very different from those taken in 1915, showing her gaunt and emaciated (though still smiling). Whether

Elsie Inglis and nurses at Hadji Abdul, September or October 1917.

the privations and difficulties of those final months hastened her end can only be speculated on, but to have endured them as uncomplainingly as she did argues great courage. It must have been a lonely battle, for there was no one of her stature or intellect out there with her. Everyone else in the unit had friends, but Dr Inglis was the commander who stood alone.

By September Elsie, aware of her own deteriorating condition, began to worry about who would take charge in an emergency. On the twenty-fourth she sent for Mary Milne, the cook, who (in spite of the lost equipment) had proved herself a valuable and steady member of the unit, and raised her to the rank of officer. Two days after that Elsie collapsed and was not thereafter able to leave her tent, though she directed the unit from her sick bed, or, on fine days, from a chair in the sun just outside it. She retained her stubborn independence, refusing to allow anyone to wait on her, and not letting anyone get away with preparing any special delicacies for her. No word of her illness appeared in her letters — indeed, on 17 October she wrote to a niece: 'We shall have about two months to refit, but one of those is my due as a holiday, *which I am going to take.*' Her attitude made the unit members believe that though she might never again be fully fit, she could not possibly be dying.

At the end of September it had appeared that the Serbs would be sent to safety, and the unit could therefore go home, but three weeks later they were still in Hadji Abdul, and the latest story was that the Serbs were to be sent to the Rumanian front after all. Elsie knew what she had to do: Mary Milne was given full instructions about who was to go home, but Dr Inglis would stay. Mrs Milne was 'very miserable' after hearing this. Dr Inglis 'was so obviously unfit to stay on, yet she would not give in.' Matters hung in the balance, but in the end she won: the Serbs went to England and to Salonica and eventually re-entered their own country in triumph.

At the end of October Elsie and the unit left for Archangel, on a train journey of nearly a fortnight. For someone in poor health it was gruelling, with no comforts (though Dr Inglis was persuaded, with much effort, to travel in a second-class compartment), and no decent food — in any case by now Elsie could barely eat. She had to lie down most of the time but insisted on dressing every morning. Twice she managed to walk on station platforms for five minutes at a time, on each occasion ending up completely exhausted. A nurse later recalled that the autocratic side of Dr Inglis, so much in evidence during times of work and heavy responsibility, was hardly seen during those weeks, when she was all kindness and charm. And Dr Gillian Ward, who would rush to the local chemist's whenever the train stopped, unsuccessfully seeking painkillers for Elsie, said 'There can never have been anyone who made more light of pain and discomfort.' (And she added, 'Next to her courage I think her affection for her Unit was her most striking characteristic, and I think she knew how deeply this was felt and reciprocated.')

There were dangers during the slow journey through revolutionary Russia — the train had to skirt Moscow because it was in the grip of a mob and thousands were killed in street fighting — and it grew ever colder, with fears that ice might close the port of Archangel before they could sail. They got there on 9 November. To reach the deck of the ship Elsie had to climb twenty feet of rope ladder; since there was no alternative, with one orderly in front and one behind, she did it.

The unit's personnel were embarked, but the precious hospital equipment still lay a mile away, marooned in a siding, for the Bolsheviks had just taken power and had called a general strike. Orderly Elsie Butler reported to Dr Inglis (who was 'lying exhausted in her bunk, and seemed to be in great pain') that there appeared to be no way of getting the equipment on board. Dr Inglis whispered to her that she must either get this done or else remain behind to guard it. Now Elsie Butler had lost her heart to the Russians as completely as Dr Inglis had lost hers to the Serbs and was sorely tempted to remain, but the work of the SWH and the wishes of Dr Inglis were paramount. She found a driver putting an engine away and begged and pleaded with him to shunt the equipment vans down to the quay. Without a word he did so. Elsie Inglis had prevailed over a nation-wide strike.

Ice breakers cleared a path, and the convoy sailed, but their dangers were not over. They were hit by one storm after another, and the convoy and escort were hopelessly scattered. The captain admitted he had no idea where he was within a hundred miles. They were near the Arctic Circle, at risk from submarines and icebergs; the pumps broke down, the engine room was flooded, and the crew was close to mutiny.

During the early part of the voyage Elsie's condition improved slightly, and she told Mary Milne, 'After each time I go down, I rise higher and higher. I shall soon be quite well again.' But then she had a relapse and suffered violent pain. Nevertheless, she insisted on going through the accounts and prepared fresh plans for a unit to join the Serbs, telling the unit she expected to be ready to set off in six weeks' time. Before departing she had sent a telegram to headquarters committee in Edinburgh: 'On our way home, everything satisfactory and all well except me, please do not arrange any meetings for me, the others will see reporters if you wish. Am going myself direct to London to report to Committee inform headquarters and relations.' She also sent a telegram to one of her sisters: 'On our way home. Have not been very well; nothing to worry about. Shall report to London, then come straight to you. Longing to see you all.' Neither message gave anyone at home cause for alarm.

The night before the ship landed at Newcastle she was in such pain she could not sleep at all, but next morning (24 November) she insisted on getting up to say goodbye to the Serbian staff. For about twenty minutes she stood, unsupported, 'her face ashen and drawn like a mask, dressed in her worn uniform coat, with the faded ribbons that had seen such good service', while each officer kissed her hand, and she said 'a few words accompanied with her wonderful smile.' Then she collapsed, but still she believed — and convinced at least some of those about her — that she would recover. She was taken to the Station Hotel and sent another telegram to her family: 'I am in bed, do not telephone for a few days.' Though this still did not sound serious, one of her nieces, Eve Simson, was sufficiently alarmed to set off for Newcastle, arriving there in the early hours of Monday morning (26 November).

Eve Simson was shocked at how 'terribly wasted' her aunt was, but Elsie gave her 'such a strong embrace that I never thought the illness was more than what might easily be cured on land, with suitable diet.' But when Dr Ward saw her she found her much worse than she had been the day before and called in another doctor as well. Still, when Elsie said goodbye to members of the unit who had not yet gone, she told them that she would be in London in a few days' time. By this time Eve had been told by the second doctor that there was little hope of her aunt living, so she phoned her mother and aunt who arrived that evening. And Elsie dictated farewell messages to members of the unit and her family.

One sister (Eva Shaw McLaren) wrote that 'it was a glorious experience to be with her those last two hours. She was emaciated almost beyond recognition, but all sense of her bodily weakness was lost in the grip one felt of the strong alert spirit, which dominated every one in the room. She was clear in her mind, and most loving to the end. The words she greeted us with were — "So I am going over to the other side." When she saw we could not believe it, she said, with a smile, "For a long time I meant to live, but now I know I am going."' To her sister 'she seemed to be entering into some great experience, for she kept repeating, "This is wonderful — but this is wonderful."' After she died, 'there remained with those that loved her only a great sense of triumph and perfect peace. The room seemed full of a glorious presence. One of us said, "This is not death; it makes one wish to follow after."'

But outside this little circle no one had an inkling of the situation. The London committee was still wondering what train she would arrive on and planning arrangements for a 'good welcome'. And then the news broke: Elsie Inglis was gone forever.

The reaction at all levels was instant and intense — the press eulogies, the Queen's letter, the lying-in-state, the crowds thick on Princes Street as the coffin passed by, and the high-and-mighty of Europe gathered at Westminster. All were paying homage to one woman at a time when the Great War was in its fourth year and millions already lay dead on the battlefields of Europe. What was it about her that so captured the public imagination?

For one thing, she was a heroine of a very British kind, her virtues those of a devotion to duty and a keen sense of responsibility. She had endured hardships and privations uncomplainingly in pursuit of her mission to succour the sick and wounded — most notably the Serbs, who had been so badly let down by their allies — and, it appeared, had sacrificed her life in so doing. She was pragmatic, a 'doer', and personally unassuming. And she had received no recognition, and considerable obstruction, from her own government.

However, her appeal transcended those aspects and was truly international. There was her sympathy and compassion, remembered by the many who knew her when she laboured on behalf of the poor and needy in Edinburgh, her vision and inspiration, her courage and energy. All these were greatly mourned and missed when she died.

DR ELSIE INGLIS.

Death of Founder of Scottish Women's Hospitals.

A REMARKABLE RECORD.

We regret to announce the death of Dr Elsie Maud Inglis, founder of the Scottish Women's Hospitals, which took place at an English port on her arrival in this country from Russia, where she had been on duty as chief medical officer of a unit of the S.W.H. attached to the Serbian Division of the Russian Army. She was born in India, where her father was in the Civil Service. She was educated abroad and at Edinburgh University, where she graduated in medicine and also took the triple qualifications of the Royal Colleges. Dr Inglis was one of the first women medical students to qualify.

The story of the last three years of Dr Elsie Inglis's life is a remarkable record of a Scotswoman's war work. Before the war Dr Inglis was a well-known woman medical practitioner in

Edinburgh, and was also known all over Scotland as prominently connected with the suffrage movement, being honorary secretary of the Scottish Federation of the National Union of Women's Suffrage Societies.

On the outbreak of war, when the union decided to suspend its political propaganda and take up war work, it was Dr Inglis who proposed the formation of the Scottish Women's Hospitals, and it was largely due to her energy and gift for organisation that this immense scheme was successfully set afoot and carried through.

Dr Inglis in Serbia.

Dr Inglis's medical war work was closely identified with Serbia. As acting commissioner for the Scottish Women's Hospitals she went

Part of the obituary of Elsie Inglis in The Bulletin.

Conclusion

The Scottish Women's Hospitals raised half a million pounds and continued their war work after their founder's death. An Elsie Inglis Memorial Hospital was started at Sallanches in the Alps for tubercular young Serbs, and an Elsie Inglis Unit went out under the London committee to aid the Serbs in Macedonia. Immediately after the war two units worked in Serbia itself. There was money enough to found a new hospital run by Serbian medical women in Belgrade, though the Balkans were so chaotic that the hospital did not open until 1929. Money was also given to Scottish women's hospitals in Edinburgh, Glasgow and Dundee. A memorial fund was started, and in 1925 the newly-built Elsie Inglis Memorial Maternity Hospital replaced The Hospice. It closed in 1988 when maternity services were reorganised, but the building was saved by a vigorous campaign and became the Elsie Inglis Nursing Home.

So much for buildings and memorials. How do we assess Elsie Inglis herself? To the modern reader her character, particularly her feminism, is a curious blend of the Victorian and the contemporary. Aspects which seemed outdated even to the young Edwardian women under her charge, like her primness about 'flirting', jar because overall her brand of feminism is so accessible. As far as she was concerned, women had the capacity to be men's equals in every possible way (barring only physical strength), and much of her life was dedicated to proving that this was so. Her impatience with women, as much as with men, who believed that the male sex had some kind of inherent superiority, is very refreshing. Perhaps she lacked empathy with women brought up to believe themselves inferior, but it made her a powerful role model. (One of her nieces, Florence Inglis, became a doctor and served at Royaumont, the Scottish Women's Hospital on the Western Front, and two other nieces were orderlies in Scottish Women's Hospitals.)

Was Elsie Inglis a happy woman? That is not an easy question to answer for, as her most substantive biographer, Margot Lawrence, found, Elsie hid behind a formidable reserve. We saw at the end of Chapter 2 that at the outbreak of war she appeared to have a full and contented life: she was as successful as a medical woman could be at that time, adored by her patients and their families, with a close network of family and friends, and part of a nationwide campaign to win women the vote. Yet there was a shadow side, the 'illness' so vaguely referred to which would kill her only a few years later.

After her death her sister wrote that the secret of her success was her 'vision': 'her life was based on a profound trust in God, and her vision was that of a follower of Christ, the vision of the kingdom of heaven upon earth.' But in fact at one point — perhaps in the wake of her father's death — she went through a crisis of faith, confessing (though not in writing) that she went to church only because she did not want to cut herself off from the religious life of her day rather than because she could find a meaning to it.

Here the unpublished, autobiographical novel provides a clue, for her heroine also went through something similar and came out the other side: 'It seemed to her as if she had been asleep and the "Celestial Surgeon" had come and "stabbed her spirit wide awake." Joy had done its work, and sorrow; responsibility had come with its stimulating spur, and the ardent delight of battle in a great crusade. New powers she had discovered in herself, new possibilities in the world around her.' And she had regained her faith: 'The Power of an Endless Life' were words that thrilled her 'with the excitement of advance, "an Endless Life" with ever new possibilities of growth and of achievement, ever greater battles to be fought for the right, and always new hopes of happiness... She began dimly to feel the "power" of the idea, the life of which she was the holder, only "part of a greater whole." Earth itself only a step in a great progression. Ever upward, ever onward, marching towards some "Divine far-off event, to which the whole creation moves.'''

Drawing on her inner resources while keeping her own counsel to come to terms with the loss of the person who meant most to her, and the desolation of the spirit that followed, was characteristic of Elsie Inglis, and she did the same when she was terminally ill. But clearly her sister was right in thinking that, by 1910 at least, her religious faith did underpin her life. At the same time the inspiration she provided to others was grounded in her own sense of worth and achievement.

How should she be rated professionally? She was not an innovator and will not be remembered for pioneering any technique or expanding existing knowledge. Even the Scottish Women's Hospitals, though much larger than any other comparable organisation, was not the only — or even the first — to send out all-women units to the front. It was, however, the most successful and well-known, and much of this must be ascribed to the high standards and example of good practice set by Dr Inglis.

Surgery was her first love, and after her death a colleague said that 'It was a pleasure to see Dr Inglis in the operating-theatre. She was quiet, calm, and collected, and never at a loss, skilful in her manipulations, and able to cope with any emergency.' Marie Agnes Davies, who had been a probationer at The Hospice from 1906 to 1908, wrote: 'She was a wonderful surgeon and her standard of asepsis so high that during the eighteen months that I was on the staff there was not a single stitch abscess, an achievement in those early days.' The high standard of asepsis comes as no surprise, for it was very much in evidence throughout her service in the war, but the praise for her surgical manner does not tally with Ellie Rendel's assessment quoted in an earlier chapter. However, the colleague and probationer saw a skilled obstetrician operating in her own accustomed environment, whereas Ellie Rendel was seeing a sick woman in her fifties with little experience of battlefield surgery working under great stress. It may be that Dr Inglis' perfectionism, so valuable in a peacetime setting, made it harder for her to cope with the chaos of war.

Was Elsie Inglis a great leader? She certainly got things accomplished. Her own sister acknowledged that 'once started in pursuit of an object, she was most reluctant to abandon it, and her gaze was so keenly fixed on the end in view, that it must be admitted she was found by some to be "ruthless" in the way in which she pushed on one side any who seemed to her to be delaying or obstructing the fulfilment of her project. There was, however, never any selfish motive prompting her; the end was always a noble one, for she had an unselfish, generous nature.'

The flaw which might make one hesitate to call her 'great' was displayed in her early threat to resign from the Bruntsfield Hospital on a point of principle and her more spectacular threat to resign from the Scottish Women's Hospitals, in both cases blind to the likely consequences of her action, and not amenable to compromise. She was perfectly capable of working within a committee structure — there is no suggestion of any serious rifts during her years as honorary secretary to the Edinburgh suffrage society and the Scottish Federation — but when it came to the crunch and she thought the committee out of step with her, then a swift and total severance had to follow. Ellie Rendel's depiction of her (admittedly in highly fraught circumstances) as a woman prone to losing her temper, fits in all too well.

But, though flawed as a leader, Elsie Inglis had the great gift of inspiring others. From the Medical College for Women to The Hospice to the Scottish Women's Hospitals, she made things happen, not only because she came up with such practical, concrete ideas, but because she believed in them so fully herself and was able to fire others with her own vision.

Elizabeth Abbott, the NUWSS organiser who later went to India and Australia to raise funds for the Scottish Women's Hospitals, related incidents which remained most strongly in her memory. Her first meeting with Elsie was in the shop in Edinburgh which had been turned into a suffrage committee room during an election and where a 'meagre fire smoked' on a dismal, grey day. To Elizabeth, 'giving away sodden handbills in the street' seemed pretty pointless. But then 'the doors swung open and Dr Inglis came into that dull place, and with her there came the very feeling of movement, vitality, action.' Elsie, appointing speakers to go to various venues that evening, finally turned to Elizabeth and told her where she would speak. '"But I must explain," I said; "I am quite 'new.' I don't speak at all. I have never spoken."… There was just the jolliest, cheeriest laugh and, "Oh, but you must speak." That was all.' Elizabeth did speak that night: 'It never occurred to me to refuse. Confidence begat confidence.'

When the suggestion came to travel to India, and Elizabeth had to be ready to leave in ten days' time, that seemed impossible to accomplish,

Crowd at the re-dedication of the memorial to Elsie Inglis at Mladenovac, Serbia.

but 'Dr Inglis was one to whom the words "can't" and "impossible" really and literally had no meaning; and those who worked with her had to "unlearn" them, and they did… I laughed with glee at the very ridiculous, fantastic impossibility of the whole thing — and promptly went!'

There is just one final question to pose. In 1917 the fame of Elsie Inglis as a doctor was so securely established that it seemed as certain to endure in history and in popular memory as had that of Florence Nightingale as a nurse. Why did it not? One explanation lies in the different futures of the nursing and medical professions. When nursing became professionalised after the First World War it was as a career for women. Medical schools, on the other hand, once again closed their doors to women students, and for a long time most medical women continued to find work only in obstetrics and gynaecology. The Scottish Women's Hospitals gave medical women responsibility and status, but it was an *ad hoc*, unofficial organisation serving other governments. The British War Office, even when forced by circumstances to recruit women doctors in the Great War, never let them near the front lines, and refused them officer status.

Unlike Florence Nightingale, Elsie Inglis did not break the mould. No matter what they had achieved during the First World War, after it was over women doctors were as marginalised as they had been before. Some SWH doctors continued the struggle through the Medical Women's Federation, but it was a long and slow road to equality. The profession may be more equal in numbers now, and women doctors can be found in many specialities, but the high-status fields like surgery are still dominated by men. To remember and to teach children about the achievements of Elsie Inglis and the Scottish Women's Hospitals would have been to acknowledge that medical women were every bit as capable as men, and Britain was not yet ready for such an acknowledgment. Has the time yet come?

INDEX

BIBLIOGRAPHY

BALFOUR, Lady Frances *Dr Elsie Inglis*, London, 1918

LAWRENCE, Margot *Shadow of Swords — A Biography of Elsie Inglis*, London, 1971

LENEMAN, Leah *In the Service of Life — The Story of Elsie Inglis and the Scottish Women's Hospitals*, Edinburgh, 1994

LENEMAN, Leah 'Medical Women at War, 1914–1918', in *Medical History*, vol 38, 1994

LENEMAN, Leah *A Guid Cause — The Women's Suffrage Movement in Scotland*, Edinburgh, 1995

MCLAREN, Eva Shaw *Elsie Inglis The Woman with the Torch*, London, 1920

MCLAREN, Eva Shaw (ed) *A History of the Scottish Women's Hospitals*, 1919

PLACES TO VISIT IN EDINBURGH

Bruntsfield Hospital, Whitehouse Loan

Dean Cemetery

Elsie Inglis Nursing Home, Spring Gardens

National War Memorial, Edinburgh Castle

Scottish National Portrait Gallery, Queen Street

St Giles Cathedral, High Street

The Hospice, 219 High Street

See leaflet *The Elsie Inglis Memorial Trail* in Edinburgh Room at Edinburgh Central Public Library

Other titles from NMS Publishing

Precious Cargo: Scots and the China trade

Robert Burns, Farmer

Tartan

Scenery of Scotland

Viking-age Gold & Silver of Scotland

The Scottish Home

Scotland's Past in Action series
Fishing & Whaling
Sporting Scotland
Farming
Spinning & Weaving
Building Railways
Making Cars
Leaving Scotland
Feeding Scotland
Going to School
Going to Church
Scots in Sickness & Health
Going on Holiday
Going to Bed
Shipbuilding
Forthcoming titles
Bicycles, Canals, Engineering, Getting Married, Iron & Steel

Anthology series
Treasure Islands
Scotland's Weather
Scottish Endings
The Thistle at War
Forthcoming titles:
Scotland & the Sea

Archive photography series
Bairns
Into the Foreground
To See Oursels
Scottish Coins

Obtainable from all good bookshops or direct from
NMS Publishing Limited, Royal Museum, Chambers Street, Edinburgh EH1 1JF.